SARA S█

One
Mother
of a
Miracle

A MOTHER'S STORY OF
LIFE, LOSS, AND LOVE

First Print Edition, 2024

Printed in China

Publishing Services: Jodi Cowles, Brandon Janous, and Rachael Mitchell (Blue Hat Publishing)
Cover Design: Tim Marshall (Blue Hat Publishing)
Interior Layout: Jodi Cowles (Blue Hat Publishing)

ISBN (print): 978-1-962674-28-7
ISBN (ebook): 978-1-962674-29-4

While the author has made every effort to provide accurate information at the time of publication, neither the publisher nor the author assumes any responsibility for errors or changes that occur after publication.

Unless otherwise noted, all scriptures come from the THE HOLY BIBLE, NEW INTERNATIONAL VERSION®, NIV® Copyright © 1973, 1978, 1984, 2011 by Biblica, Inc.® Used by permission. All rights reserved worldwide.

Scripture quotations marked (ESV) are from The ESV® Bible (The Holy Bible, English Standard Version®), © 2001 by Crossway, a publishing ministry of Good News Publishers. Used by permission. All rights reserved.

Contents

Dedication   1

Part One   3

1. It Started With a Fire   5

2. The Making of a Miracle   9

3. The Birth   17

4. 1200 seconds   23

5. HIE   31

6. Turning a Corner   41

Part Two   49

7. Waiting for the Other Shoe to Drop   51

8. A Miracle Born Again   57

9. NICU Alumni   61

10. Is This a Joke?   67

11. Fighting for Fertility   73

12. An Unmentioned Birthday   77

Part Three   79

13. Two Pink Lines   81

14. Back on the Battlefield   87

15. Tiny Fighter   95

16. Down but Not Out   102

17. The End of the Beginning   111

18. Picking Up the Pieces   122

Part Four   131

19. In Sickness and In Health   133

20. It Takes a Village   137

21. Golfing With Giraffes   141

22. Faith Through Failure   145

23. Calling Over Comfort   151

24. Bowen Walker Foundation   155

25. A God-Sized Plan   159

26. A Web of Grace   163

27. One Mother of a Miracle   171

Acknowledgements   177

I dedicate this book to my husband, as we walk hand in hand on this journey. To our boys, for making me a mama, and always teaching me as we grow together. To every NICU parent who finds a piece of themselves, and every loss parent who relates, I write this book for you. To every person who picks up these pages, thank you for giving myself, and my book, a chance.

Content warning: This book contains potentially triggering subject matter, including discussions of trauma, infertility, NICU stays, panic attacks, PTSD, and infant loss.

Part One

CHAPTER ONE

It Started With a Fire

It all started with a fire. In October of 2016, lightning struck in the mountains, starting a wildfire and filling the surrounding air with smoke. A dark, thick haze settled all around us, and the smell of burnt leaves lingered in your nose. North Georgia was in flames, and at this point over 200 acres of mountainous forest had been burnt. The smoke began to spread, and soon as far as the eye could see were clouds of grey hovering in the air around you. I've suffered from asthma my entire life, so it did not take long before I began to feel the consequences of the heavy, smoke-filled air.

I knew exactly what to do in the event of an attack; however, as I'd gotten older, the need for an inhaler had lessened until I had finally stopped using one altogether. As I shuffled my way through the murky fumes that filled the air around me, it became harder to take a deep breath. Wheezing began. The rattle of my lungs was becoming more frequent, creating a musical addition to my breathing. I was 30 weeks pregnant with my first child, and physically miserable: grunting as I attempted to get up and down, a wheezing rattle generating from my asthma, and continuing to suffer from a three-day-long, ongoing pounding migraine.

Like most young moms-to-be, I decided the best thing to do was call in an expert—my own mom. While I waited for her to answer the phone, I could hear my lungs rattling between rings. Finally, she picked up. I began ranting my list of ailments. My head still hurt. My chest was tight.

I was a million months pregnant and swollen. The list went on and on. As she listened, the level of concern in her voice began to rise. As a mother of three herself, she knew what signs to look for in pregnancy, and she urged me to call the doctor. She informed me that oftentimes in pregnancy, headaches can mean high blood pressure; even though I have chronic migraines, it was better to be safe than sorry. She began to tell me about our family history of preeclampsia and urged that at the very least I needed to have my inhaler refilled.

Later that afternoon, I shuffled my way to the car, drove to the pharmacy, and picked up my new inhaler. While I was there, as a precaution and to ease my mother's mind, I sat down in the blood pressure machine chair. I slid my arm in the cuff, remembering how much I loved to play with these machines as a child. As I pressed the button to start the test, I sat still, confident that I was fine. I felt fine. If I could get my inhaler, my asthma would get under control, my headaches would all go away, and everything would be okay. The machine hummed to life, the cuff began to tighten, and I waited. As the test carried on, my fingers began to tingle, falling asleep even. Finally, the air began to release. This was it. I'd be able to ease my mom's mind, grab my prescription, and head home to relax on the couch. Little did I know, this one test would drastically change the rest of my pregnancy.

145/90. The numbers popped up, and I immediately knew they were high. I was an active, healthy 21-year-old woman. I had recently left my job in preparation for the new baby and lived a simple, happy life with my husband and dog. Why did I have such high blood pressure? A mother's intuition is rarely wrong, and I was living this realization firsthand with my own mom. She was right. Again. Thankfully. Something was wrong with me, and I needed help. My mind began racing at a million miles an hour as anxiety and panic set in. My chest hurt. My hands, although no longer tingling, were clammy and wet. An internal heat began to rise in my body as I stared at the numbers on the screen. Endless questions flooded my mind. Was the baby okay? Was I okay? What now???

I picked up the phone, my fingers shaking as I dialed the number for my doctor for the third time that day. "Come in *right away*," they told me. Their office was supposed to close in 30 minutes, but due to the severity of the situation, they stayed open to see me. I wasted no time at all and went right in, frantically calling my husband and mom to fill them in on what had just transpired. By the time I got to the doctor's, my blood pressure numbers were even higher than before.

Blood samples were drawn, urine samples were collected, the baby was checked on, and immediate follow-up appointments were scheduled. I was 30 weeks pregnant, 21 years old, and officially on high blood pressure medication and put on bed rest. Induction was put on the table, and my doctor confirmed that I would not be making it to my due date. I was diagnosed with hypertension and monitored extremely closely.

The next seven weeks were the longest weeks of the whole pregnancy. Every two to three days I journeyed to either the OBGYN or the hospital. My life consisted of countless trips to the doctor, numerous non-stress tests to make sure the baby was okay, and a *lot* of time spent watching TV on the couch. We set the date for induction for my 37th week of pregnancy and prayed I would safely remain pregnant that long. Our goal was set, and it was my job to try and ensure we met it. At each appointment, we were told to pack a bag and prepare to be sent directly to the hospital depending on how my body was acting at that moment. We never knew which appointment would be the last, we had no idea how far I would make it, or what that meant for me or my baby.

Little did I know that this would ultimately save my baby's life. God knew what He was doing; He was in control. Isn't it amazing how God's plan can use something as simple as a forest fire and in turn save a life? Oftentimes it is so hard to see the big picture and trust in His plan entirely. I was frustrated that I was on bed rest. I was tired of going to the doctor multiple times a week. I hated that I had to check my blood pressure every few hours. But I did. Had the fire not triggered my asthma, we would not have discovered my high blood pressure when we did. My life would not be the way it is today. Because we caught it when we did, I am able to share what happened next.

This is just the beginning of God's plan. What seemed at the time like an insignificant forest fire turned into the beginning of a testimony more powerful than I could ever have imagined. His handiwork became evident as He got to work weaving His web, cultivating my story, and preparing me to become one mother of a miracle.

CHAPTER TWO

The Making of a Miracle

Six o'clock in the evening on December 4, 2016. At 37 weeks and 2 days, my husband and I checked into the labor and delivery unit at our local hospital in preparation for what would end up being a long, excruciating induction. I was filled with nervous anticipation and overly excited. This was it. No turning back. Soon we would be holding our perfect baby boy. I remember thinking to myself that there would be no issues. In roughly 24 hours I would be pushing, welcoming my son into this world, and then sharing him with all of our family and friends. The staff members at the hospital were so friendly. They made me feel calm. They made me feel safe and reassured. I signed paperwork and went over risks. The Cervidil, a medication used to prepare my body for labor, was placed, and I was well on my way to having a baby.

At the time of the birth, Zach, my husband, worked nights, so we had planned for him to go in to work that night, knowing we should be safe for a little while. We had planned for my mom to meet me at the hospital so I would not be alone, and were ready for our perfect labor and delivery experience. Soon, Zach left for work, and my mom arrived to settle into the spacious labor suite and stay the night with me. The hospital room was gorgeous. The labor and delivery wing at our hospital had only been open a little over two months, and everything was shiny and brand new. The beds were as comfortable as hospital beds can be, the TVs were new and big, and don't even get me started on the bathrooms. The walk-in showers had bench seating and a waterfall shower head. I felt as if I had checked myself into a spa, and I was ready to get this show on the road. I tried to sleep but was just too excited; instead I dozed on and off, thinking and dreaming about the day to come, while the Cervidil did its work preparing my body for labor.

After a mostly boring and uncomfortable but somewhat restful night's sleep, I opened my eyes to see the sun peeking out from behind the clouds through my hospital room window. It was a new day, *the* day. Baby day. Picking up my phone, I saw it was just a few minutes past seven o'clock on the morning of December 5. Not long after waking up, I was greeted by the woman who would be my nurse for the next 12 hours, followed shortly by my doctor. Together they came into my room, confirmed the Cervidil had done its job overnight, and decided it was time to break my water. A pop, followed by a gush of fluid, created a very uncomfortable mess in my bed, but that did not matter because we were one step closer to having our son in our arms. This was it, I was in labor.

I excitedly called Zach at work to tell him we were on the right track, and informed him that he should hurry back to the hospital because we were about to start Pitocin. The clock was ticking, and although progression was slow, my contractions were roughly two to three minutes apart. In what seemed like no time at all, Zach walked back into my hospital room, still in uniform from the night before, with the biggest smile spread across his face. The day we had dreamt of for the last nine months was finally here, and we were beyond ready to have this baby.

The next 14 hours were the most physically painful hours of my entire life. An indescribably intense type of pain radiated throughout my body. I was drenched in sweat, my hands numb from the tightness of my grip on anything and everything I could find, and the inability to focus on anything around me left me in tears. Like the stubborn woman I am, I held out as long as humanly possible before requesting pain medication. I put all my focus and energy into my breathing, attempting to just make it through the next contraction. Seconds turned into minutes which turned into hours, and with each tick of the clock, the pain increased, the length of my contractions seemed longer, and the time in between became so short I was constantly left breathless. I began to realize that what I was experiencing was not right.

Uterine tachysystole. In laymen's terms for all the non-medical people like me, uterine tachysystole is hyperstimulation, or excessive duration and intensity of contractions. The list of potential outcomes of uterine tachysystole seems endless, and includes the possibilities of uterine rupture, placental abruption, and serious negative impact on the baby. Before beginning Pitocin, my doctor had gone over the side effects it can have, including what I was currently experiencing. The likelihood, however, of experiencing these extreme side effects was astronomically low, and just as quickly as I heard about the possibility of them, they exited my head.

My contractions continued to get longer and longer, followed by less and less time in between. Eventually, I was having contractions lasting upwards of 90 seconds, followed by a short two- to three-second rest and recovery period. The cycle of excruciatingly long, painful contractions repeated over and over, my only relief coming when the Pitocin was withdrawn. Throughout the day, nurses consistently had to turn down the amount of Pitocin I was receiving. With each decrease in the medicine, I breathed easier. The issue we continued to run into was that my body also slowed down the labor, coming almost completely to a halt. The endless carousel continued, mediated through my IV. Pitocin increased, uterine tachysystole returned. Pitocin decreased, labor stalled. Over and over again, we tried and failed to find the sweet spot for labor.

Each hour got a little more painful, but I knew this meant it was just one minute closer to holding our baby.

I finally gave in and asked for pain meds. As the IV entered my blood stream, the pain began to melt away. For the next hour, I felt great. My mom and I played cards to pass the time. Sooner than anticipated, however, the pain meds wore off, and the harsh contractions returned in full force. Once again, my Pitocin was turned off because I wasn't getting breaks in between contractions. We started a new set of IV medications in an attempt to increase Pitocin and get back on track with my labor. They didn't work. Excruciating pain radiated throughout my body as I was once again back at square one. I felt like I couldn't breathe. I felt like I couldn't do it any longer. Frustration began to set in, and with each failed attempt, I continued to deny the need for an epidural, stubbornly convincing myself that I could do this. I could deal with the pain.

After 12 hours, I was exhausted. Sweat dripped down from my head. My arms and hands were sore and numb from squeezing through the pain—my husband swears to this day that I broke his finger. At seven o'clock in the evening, I finally gave in and begged for an epidural. I'd held off as long as possible; I'd tried to do it all on my own. Before going to the hospital, I'd always said the second they offered me an epidural, I was taking it, no questions asked. I chose to hold off that day, however, knowing I needed to wait. I knew I would need it later, and boy, was I right.

My epidural was placed, and immediately I felt better. Instant relief. For the first time in nearly 12 hours, I felt as if I could relax, I could finally exhale. I was calm and able to breathe again. The next hour and a half were the most magical moments of my labor. For the first time since that morning, I could smile, joke around, and dream of the future that would arrive sooner than I realized.

As my breath softened, my mind shifted back to earlier that year. My little sister and lifelong best friend, Jessie, had made the brave and exciting decision to join the United States Army. She'd left for basic training in October. I was heartbroken that she would miss her nephew's birth, but so proud of her for her choice to serve. She was coming home soon for Christmas, and we couldn't count down the seconds fast enough.

A few minutes after I received my epidural, my mom walked excitedly back into my room. After a long day and a half at the hospital with me, she had run out for a few hours. She'd gotten my youngest sister, only 12 at the time, dinner, and run home to check the mail, where she'd found a letter addressed to me. It was from Jessie. She had written me from boot camp, and it could not have arrived at a better time. Beaming with excitement, my mom waved the letter in her hand. Reading her letters always made us happy, and it's safe to say I needed a good distraction from the pain. We sat around the room as my mom read it aloud.

For the most part, my sister had written about what they had been doing and learning and how excited she was to come home for Christmas. About three quarters of the way through the letter, however, there was a Bible verse. It stood alone with no explanation, no reason included for its existence. It was just . . . there. When my mom read it, I immediately started to sob. I knew I needed to hear it, but did not know why. It struck me in such a way that I couldn't help but know that God was speaking to me through Jessie and through her letter.

For his anger lasts only a moment, but his favor lasts a lifetime; weeping may stay for the night, but rejoicing comes in the morning (Psalm 30:5).

do great in the delivery room and just remember that pain is temporary, but you are looking forward to literally a life full of love. Also even though you will be very tired during those first couple of days & nights with him, keep on pushing through and know that it will get better. I've learned a whole lot about that recently. "The pain that you are feeling cannot compare to the joy that is coming." I can't believe how much our lives are changing and I know we'll both be going all over the place (figuratively & literally) over not only the next few months, but the years to come. but always remember that you were my first best friend and that will never ever change. I am always here for you and will encourage you through every step of life. I am so excited to be an aunt and I will always strive to teach, love, support & guide all through his life. I love you and I know you will be an amazing mom.

Love Always,
(Auntie) Jessie

Soon, though, I had dismissed these thoughts, although I still could not wrap my head around why it would mean so much. The contractions and the excitement of holding our baby made me forget about the verse momentarily. The nurse had checked me right after receiving my epidural and determined that I was nine centimeters dilated.

The excitement of Jessie's letter, the progression of my long, excruciating labor, and the relief I was finally receiving left me in a euphoric state of peace. I was impatiently waiting to hold my son, while understandably nervous about having to push an entire human out of my body in the very near future. The nurses came in and told me it was almost time to push, since I was nearing ten centimeters, but asked if I would be okay to wait a few minutes in order to make sure that baby was where he needed to be. They explained that they wanted to ensure a safe and quick delivery. Confidently, I said yes. In my heart, regardless of the anxiety and impatience, I just knew it wasn't time.

Immediately after my nurse exited my room, my phone began to ring. Jessie's name was displayed across the screen. For the first time in 42 days, I was able to talk to my sister! Tears of joy welled up big in my eyes and immediately began to flow down my face. Excitedly, I answered. "Jessie, I'm in labor!" I cried out to her. It was an event we had talked about since we were little girls, a memory so special, a moment I was finally able to share with my sister. My sister's unit wasn't supposed to get their phones that day. In fact, they had only been given their phones twice in the 41 days before that. It was a God thing. My talk with Jessie, although short, gave me the confidence I needed and would need as the night progressed. I felt calm, I felt ready. I could do this. The nurse came back in, and it was go time. This was it. I was ready to push. My life was about to change in a big way; I just didn't know how big God's plan was yet.

CHAPTER THREE

The Birth

This was it. For almost 26 hours I had prepared both my mind and my body for this moment. As I entered into the final steps toward bringing our little boy into the world, I began to reflect on the time spent to get here. "Wow, these past nine months have flown by," I thought to myself. I had been in active labor for over 12 hours by that point, and finally it was time to push.

1–2–3–*push.*

1–2–3–*push.*

1–2–3–*push.*

1–2–3 . . . stop??? *Stop?!* Why was I stopping?! I was doing so good! I was ready! I was motivated! I was *finally* about to become a mom and meet the baby I had dreamt of my entire life. My nurse, Brandy, stared at the monitor, a concerned yet calm look on her face. She called in someone for a second opinion. *A second opinion on what??*

There I was, spread-eagled, heart pounding, waiting for a second opinion. One nurse entered, then another. Next thing I knew, a swarm of nurses was rushing into my room. Zach and my mom, who were once standing by my head, were now pushed into a corner, a look of fear and panic spreading equally across their faces. The nurses all stared at the monitors; periodically, someone would adjust the straps on my belly before going back to the monitors again. What was everyone looking at? Was I having bad contractions again? Compared to the contractions I was feeling earlier, these didn't seem so bad. *Thank God for this epidural,* I thought to myself. "Flip over. Roll to your side. Get on your hands and knees." *What the heck am I doing?! Nobody told me about* this *part of labor!!* I frantically flipped and flopped, rolled and rocked, still not knowing exactly what was happening. I knew something was wrong, but was still unsure of exactly what, and then I saw her. My doctor was the next person to rush into my room. *God bless my doctor. And Brandy. I brag about them to everyone. They're my angels. Our angels.*

"I'm going to watch the monitor for a minute, and we may go for an emergency C-section," she said to me. There it was. Emergency. What was going on?! I remember asking if everything was okay. If my son was okay. Nobody would answer me. Zach and my mom continued to stand frozen together in the corner. They watched in panic as their wife and daughter, as well as their son and grandson, lay helpless in fear just a few feet away. Almost immediately, the call was made and the clock started. We were going for an emergency C-section. This baby needed to get out, and get out now.

Panic set in. Where was Zach?! Where was my mom?! My doctor got down to my level. She looked me in the eye and held my hand. "I need you to trust that I have you and I have your baby. I need you to trust me." I can still hear her voice to this day. Wheels were up, and there we went. I lay on my bed trying to breathe, watching hospital lights pass by on the ceiling overhead as I was rushed to the operating room to begin emergency surgery in an attempt to save my son's life.

The anesthesiologist introduced himself and told me they would be putting me under. Never in my life had I had surgery, and the idea of being put under is my biggest fear. I even refused to get my wisdom teeth pulled until I was 27 because of my fear of being put under. However, in this moment of panic and chaos, I was calm. I didn't protest or fight because I knew I didn't have time. I lay there waiting to be put under, waiting to fall asleep. Inhale. My chest shook with fear as it began to rise. Exhale. My chest fell, forcefully attempting to relax. I was still awake. The anesthesia would kick in soon. Inhale. A little gentler this time. Exhale. Less forceful as I let go. Surely I'd be asleep soon.

But it didn't happen. I was still awake, aware of the chaos all around me. Refocusing, I shifted my thoughts away from the anesthesia and lay still, now waiting for the morphine they'd given me to kick in. Waiting for my body to go numb. But it didn't happen. I could still feel everything. "Is she under?" I overheard my doctor ask, wondering herself if the anesthetic worked. "Not yet, I need a minute," responded the anesthesiologist. "I don't have a minute" were the next words to come out of her mouth.

In that second, I knew the true severity of the situation I had found myself in. "I don't feel anything, just go!" I yelled to her. I didn't care about how much it would hurt. The consequences for my life meant nothing to me, because in that moment, I faced life or death: the life or the death of my child. Nothing could stop me. No fear of the pain of what it would feel like, or what was to come. I knew it was now or never, and I chose now. I chose him.

Cut one. *Hold still.* Cut two. *Don't move.* Cut three. *This is for him.* Cut four. *You can do this.* "Did you feel that?" She had begun the incision. *"Nope!"* I confidently yelled through the pain. I felt everything. I could count the incision marks. In that moment, I chose my baby over myself.

The cutting, pulling, and tugging continued. My body finally began to go numb. He was in the birth canal, and he had to come back out. I focused on lying still and quiet, afraid to move or make a noise. Shivering. Why was I shivering? Adrenaline and anxiety had taken over. My arm began to shake uncontrollably on the table beside me. No matter how hard I tried, it would not lie still. *Please, God, let us be okay. Let my son be okay.*

Nine minutes and five seconds later, Sawyer Gray Schneider was born. The doctor pulled him out of my stomach, quickly passing him to the NICU nurse standing on the opposite side of me. Silence. No crying. No wiggling. Stillness. There was no pulse. There was no heartbeat. My son. My whole world. Dead. Unalive. Born, but not alive.

"No heartbeat. No pulse." The words echoed throughout my brain as I heard them for the first time out loud. *What do you mean you cannot find a heartbeat?! What do you mean he has no pulse!?* He was okay only a few minutes ago. How could everything change so fast!? Alarms began to go off in my head. I was alone. I was terrified. My eyes squeezed tightly shut, and in that moment, I did the only thing I could think to do. I began to pray.

*Cry, cry, **cry**. Please, God, let him cry!!* Silence. I heard nothing. Instead, the room erupted into an organized frenzy as nurses, respiratory therapists, and doctors frantically jumped into action, attempting resuscitation. Waves of blue scrubs scattered all around me as I longed for just a glimpse of my son, for a sliver of existence to erupt from his small, lifeless body.

One set of nurses aided my doctor as she began to put me back together. The physical pain had completely abandoned my body, adrenaline peaking, as I craned my neck towards the second set of scrubs present in the operating room: the NICU team. Like a well-oiled machine, countless doctors, nurses, and respiratory therapists began to attempt resuscitation. Helplessly, I lay awake on the table of the operating room as they tried and failed to get my boy back.

For 20 minutes resuscitation was attempted, and in that time I gave all that I was, all that I had over to God and I prayed. I wanted to cry, but I couldn't. I wanted to scream, but a tiny whisper in my head told me not to let anyone know I was still awake. Instead, I prayed. Never in my life had I experienced prayer the way I did on that cold operating room table. Lying helpless as my insides were still being put back together, I didn't curse God. I didn't even ask why. Instead, I felt an overwhelming sense of peace: indescribable, overwhelming peace that only comes in the presence of God. Consciously breathing in, I gathered my thoughts as best I could. As I slowly and deliberately breathed out, whispers of prayer began to leave my lips. With absolute sincerity, I thanked God for each doctor, nurse, and specialist involved in our care. I thanked Him immensely for the ability to grow, carry, and love our son for the past nine months, acknowledging the joy I had experienced as I intimately got to know him within my womb. I prayed for Zach, my strong, loving, amazing husband. We'd only gotten married 14 months ago; how could I do this to him?! Trembling, I began to pray for the strength to explain to him what was happening. What had happened. I prayed that he didn't hate or resent me for allowing this to happen to *our son*. Our family. My family.

What about our families!? Our parents. Our sisters. My youngest sister was only 12, just a kid herself. Gently, I shifted my prayer to our families, praying that their hearts would heal from this loss. With each unsuccessful attempt at resuscitation, I prayed it wouldn't be the last. I prayed they wouldn't give up on him. On us. I prayed for a miracle.

Time was simultaneously standing still and flying by as I prayed and listened. Listened and prayed. No heartbeat, no pulse: Words forever ingrained into my soul. Humbly, I prayed for the outcome I had been facing, yet did not want to accept: leaving the hospital without my baby. With each second that passed, I cried out to God, declaring that even if I was alone, He was still good. Even without the baby I had spent my whole life praying over. Even without the child my husband and I had excitedly spent the past nine months preparing for. Even without the son

I had fallen in love with the day I found out he existed. Above all else, He was still good. Over and over, I listened and prayed, prayed and listened, knowing good and well with each passing moment that I was praying for a real-life miracle.

No heartbeat. No pulse. *Please, God, let him live. Save him. Save us.*

CHAPTER FOUR

1200 Seconds

Twenty minutes. 1200 seconds. Finally, it happened. A heartbeat. A miracle. Unexplainable joy. Tears flowed down my face, soaking my gown. After so many failed attempts, my son's heart had begun to beat again. My son was *alive*! *Thank You, God!*

The anesthesiologist walked over to me. Getting down on my level, he looked me in the eye and said, ***"Your son is alive."*** Over the course of those 20 minutes, I had asked him repeatedly if he was okay, and for the first time, he was able to give me the answer I had previously been begging for him to give. Admittedly, he told me that he did not know much, but what he did know was that they had finally found a heartbeat. It was confirmation of what I had overheard from the NICU team, and once again, it was the greatest news of all time.

The rest of the surgery was a blur. I wanted nothing more than to leave the operating room and tell Zach the good news. I wanted to jump up off the table and go be with my boy. With my family. The tears that once refused to fall were racing down my face, relief leaving my body and joy erupting in my soul. *Thank you, God!* ***Thank you, God!!!*** My prayers continued as the team stabilized my baby on a ventilator and wheeled him off to the NICU. Almost immediately after their exit, I saw a familiar face. Dressed in scrubs, hair tied back and tears in her eyes, I saw her. My own mom. For the first time since they were pushed aside in the delivery room, I was not alone.

Tears ran down her cheeks as a mixture of worry, shock, and fear spread across her face. In my entire life, I could count on one hand the number of times I had seen my mom cry. She didn't hide her emotions, but instead always stood tall through the storms of life, a beautiful figure of strength and resilience. As she came closer to me, I felt the love she carried in a whole new way: the love of a mother. The feelings and emotions I had just experienced with my own son, I now saw firsthand through the eyes of my own mother. I love her, I thought. I am so thankful for her. She *really* loves me, too. In that moment, I felt so much joy. So much peace. As tears stained her cheeks, her hand running through my hair and whispers of "I'm so sorry" escaping her lips, I looked up at her and recited something from the letter Jessie had written us. *"Weeping may stay for the night, but rejoicing comes in the morning"* (Psalm 30:5). In that moment, I had no other words. Instead, the verse that Jessie wrote was ingrained in my heart forever, constantly replaying in my mind.

I told my mom that God was watching over us. I began to explain to her about my prayers, and the peace surrounding me, holding me close. With as much detail as possible, I began to tell her what had happened during the surgery, and confidently told her that everything was going to be okay. Together, we sat and watched through hopeful eyes as the doctors sewed me back up; I was eager to return to my room to face the world. To face my husband, whose biggest fear had just come true; my husband, who just days ago had told me he was terrified of the *thought* of an emergency C-section, much less the actual event.

The clock ticked on, seconds turning into minutes, moving slower than ever before. Anticipation increasing with each passing moment as Zach and I sat in my room, waiting to hear something, anything. *Is he okay?* I must have asked that question about a million times.

"Mr. and Mrs. Schneider?" a familiar voice asked as a man I had never seen entered my room. He was dressed in a suit and tie, and I began to search my brain for how I recognized his voice. He was the hospital's neonatologist. He had been at a Christmas party when he received a phone call from the operating room about a non-responsive infant. For the 20 minutes that Sawyer lay lifeless on the table, this doctor was on speakerphone. I'd heard him repeatedly directing his staff not to give up, telling them that he was on the way.

He walked into our room, gently introducing himself to Zach and myself. A mixture of hope and fear began to creep into our minds. Maybe we would get some answers to the questions flooding our heads. Did we actually want those answers? Would we like what he was about to say?

The doctor began to speak, telling us a little more about what had transpired in the operating room. Sawyer was born with no pulse and no heartbeat. Resuscitation efforts took 20 minutes. After going over the things we already knew, he began to tell us about the things we had not yet heard. Would he survive? If he survived, what would his quality of life be, if any? Chests tight and breaths held, Zach and I squeezed each other's hands. Sawyer was given a 12 percent chance of survival. *If* he were to survive, his quality of life, given the injury to his brain, would more than likely be unfavorable. He might never walk. He might never talk. He might never eat on his own, run, jump, or play. As gently as possible, he finished by telling us that we might be faced with a decision no parent would ever want to make: There was a possibility we would have to make a decision to discontinue care.

As the news we'd just been told began to sink in, we were informed that only two hospitals in the state of Georgia offered a therapy that gave him a fighting change: cooling therapy. Sawyer would soon be transferred to a different hospital, and if he successfully arrived within three hours of birth, he would be able to be placed on a cooling mat. This mat would cool his internal temperature drastically and, if it worked, might help his body heal. At last, the words we had anxiously been waiting on left his lips: "Do you want to see your son?"

Yes. Finally, I would be able to see Sawyer. *We* would be able to see Sawyer. Neither Zach nor I had been able to see him yet, and with the news we had just received, we knew there was a possibility this would be the first and last time we got to see him alive. We called in my nurse and told her the plan. I was ready and determined. Less than an hour had passed since my surgery, and I knew the countdown to Sawyer's departure was quickly ticking away. With every muscle in my body, I began to pull myself up in bed. My legs were flung heavily to the side, and I began to shift my weight into a wheelchair. No amount of pain would hold me back, because I was going to the NICU to see my son, and nobody was going to stop me.

Zach and I held hands as my nurse steered my wheelchair. Side by side, we journeyed through the halls of the labor and delivery wing before arriving in front of the heavy double doors marking the entrance to the Neonatal Intensive Care Unit. Our future lay just beyond those double doors, a world of answers we would soon receive, whether we were ready for them or not.

The very first time I saw my son, he had been earthside for over an hour. Sawyer lay in a bed, tucked into a private room on the main hall of the NICU, and was surrounded by a swarm of nurses, therapists, and other hospital employees. Tubes and wires covered his body, and he was breathing only by the help of a ventilator. I had never held him, I had never touched him, but for the first time I was able to see him. I just looked at him. He was bruised and purple from 20 minutes of resuscitation efforts. His skin was not pink like that of a normal baby; instead, he was pale and gray. Doctors and nurses were crowded around in his tiny room, rushing around as they both cared for him and prepared for his exit in a second attempt at saving his life.

As I was wheeled closer, the neonatologist reappeared beside me. He showed me what looked like a twitch in Sawyer's eye, and explained that he was having seizures, a side effect from the damage caused to his brain. Aside from the small movement caused by the seizures, he was still. My baby didn't move. He didn't cry or make a noise. As I began to scan down his body, I noticed his umbilical cord was gone. In its place were wires: peripherally inserted central catheters, or PICC lines. He was so lifeless, yet so beautiful. So gray, yet so vibrant. So heartbreakingly ill, yet so joyfully my miracle. One of the first things I noticed was his gorgeous head full of hair. Everything I ever wanted was laying right in front of me, and I couldn't hold him. I couldn't hug or kiss or mother him.

"Can I touch him?" I sheepishly asked a nearby nurse. Much to my delight, she said yes, so long as I was careful not to disturb the array of wires and tubes working to keep him alive. Overjoyed, Zach and I reached out to hold his hand. We were allowed to hold his hand as long as we were not in the way of the doctors and nurses, and for the first time since his birth, time stood still in a positive way.

The transport team quickly arrived to take Sawyer to his new hospital. One at a time, they introduced themselves to Zach and myself before jumping into action, preparing my tiny, sick boy for the journey ahead of him. I nervously kept an eye on the time. I did not ever want them to go, but knew if they did not hurry, Sawyer's chance of survival would plummet. So instead, I sat quietly to the side as they got everything prepared and ready to leave—to leave me. My baby, my husband, my family. They were leaving, and I was staying. This was not how I had imagined the "best day of my life."

As the team finalized plans for his departure, the neonatologist told Zach and I more about Sawyer's "injury." Once again, were told he was going to Emory Midtown, where he would remain until further notice. We were reminded that although he was currently alive, his transport was not guaranteed to be successful, and if it was, his quality of life could not yet be measured.

After what seemed like an eternity and also the blink of an eye, the team to take Sawyer to Emory was ready to go. This was it. I had to say goodbye not only to Sawyer, but also to Zach as he went to be with our son. Before they left, I took a picture of Sawyer on the bed in the NICU. *The most beautiful picture I have ever seen,* I thought to myself. A treasured memory forever, it constantly reminds me of how far we have come, the blessings we have received, and the miracles we have witnessed along the way. The time we had with Sawyer in a room bustling with people and unknowns was so special. Left behind was an empty silence populated only by anxieties and fears, and a future full of questions.

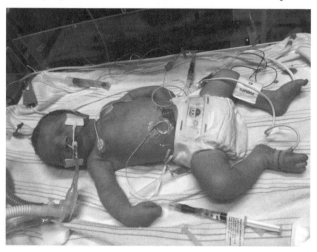

Zach, Sawyer, and the transfer team exited the NICU, turned down the long hallway to the right of the lobby, and disappeared right before my eyes. My nurse, Brandy, and I turned towards the left and began our journey back to my room. As we turned the corner and entered my room, I was met with the sea of family who had all excitedly been waiting for Sawyer's birth. For the first time since before he was born,

I saw Zach's parents, his sister, and my dad. My mom stood brave and strong alongside them, and together we held hands and began to fill in all of the blanks for them. We explained more about his birth, and I shared what the neonatologist had explained to Zach and myself and informed them all about the transfer that was currently in progress. With tears in our eyes and hope in our hearts, we gathered together and prayed. We prayed for Sawyer. We prayed for Zach. We prayed for the medical team surrounding them, and the future that lay ahead of us.

We decided on the best course of action for the remainder of the night, and agreed to take it one step at a time. The first step we decided was that Zach's family would leave, gather a few necessities, and head to Atlanta to be with Zach and Sawyer. There was a possibility Sawyer would not survive the night, and we all knew Zach did not need to be alone. My best friend Kayla had taken my youngest sister, Rachel, to get dinner and then back home for the night, and shortly after I was settled back in my room, my mom followed them. My dad walked my in-laws and mom outside before returning. He firmly planted himself in the chair of my hospital room, pulled out his computer, and set up camp. Without him speaking a word, we both knew he was staying. His little girl, his firstborn, had just endured tragedy, and there was nothing that would pull him away from me.

The next few hours, my hospital room turned into a revolving door as we were met with nurses, doctors, and specialists coming to check on me and my stitches. As many questions as possible were answered, and on more than one occasion, we bowed our heads and prayed together. People who just hours before were complete strangers began to open their hearts to me one by one, sharing their faith and testimonies and praying deep and intimate prayers for my family.

I knew I needed sleep, but the questions about my family's future kept me awake. I still had not heard from Zach, the ambulance ride to Emory taking what seemed like forever. "Surely, they've arrived," I repeated over and over to my dad. We sat in my hospital room, anxiously awaiting Zach's text to tell me they had made it safely. "No news is good news," we both repeated, convincing each other and ourselves with each passing moment. Around one o'clock in the morning, my phone dinged. Finally. My heart began to race as I saw Zach's name illuminating the dark hospital room. Zach's message explained that they had arrived safely. He told us that Sawyer was in their NICU, and for the first time since their arrival, he had been taken back to see him. As I was reading the first message, a second came through. It was a picture.

Pink. Sawyer was ***pink***. Not purple or gray. Not pale. Pink. He looked so different. He actually looked like a living, breathing, *alive* baby. Tension left my body, and for the first time since my boys had left the hospital, I was able to exhale. Gently, I put my phone down, closed my eyes, and immediately drifted off to sleep. A sense of calm overcame me, giving me peace that things might be okay. Things would be okay. God was in control. That picture was the only reason I got any sleep that night.

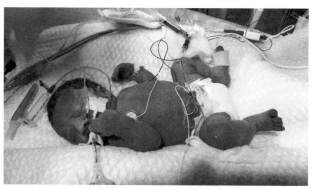

CHAPTER FIVE

HIE

It had been two days since Sawyer was born, and I was finally discharged to go see him. After a quick trip by my house for clothes and other necessities, my mom and I were on our way to the hospital in Atlanta. For the first time since my son was born, I would be reunited with him and my husband. My little family would be together as one.

As we were driving down the interstate, my phone began to ring. Zach was calling. Every time his name popped up on my phone, I held my breath. Was this it? Would I like the words coming from my husband's voice on the other end of the line?

"They rescanned Sawyer's brain in search of possible brain bleeds," he began. The next few seconds seemed to drag on for years. I could hear the pounding of my heart as I anxiously awaited what would come next. "They did not find any brain bleeds."

Zach's voice began to crack with tears as he told me the news. The moment was frozen in time as I sat in the passenger seat of my mom's SUV. *No brain bleeds.* A wave of emotions hit me like a tsunami, and I burst into tears. "No brain bleeds," I repeated to my mom with tear-soaked cheeks.

You could feel the relief through her exhale. "Thank you, Jesus," she repeated over and over as we continued the drive. The rest of the trip to Atlanta seemed like a blur, until finally we turned into the entrance at Emory. Zach met me outside with a wheelchair, excitedly helping me get into it, and we began the journey to the NICU. I remember the feeling of relief, of joy, of God's presence. I was still unable to hold Sawyer or kiss him or love all over him, but I was there, and that was more than enough.

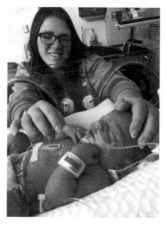

The doctor overseeing Sawyer's case came out and introduced himself to my mom and me. He began to explain to us more of what had happened to Sawyer, and for the first time, we heard his official diagnosis: hypoxic-ischemic encephalopathy, or HIE for short. HIE is brain damage affecting the central nervous system, caused by a lack of oxygen before, during, or after birth. The neonatologist began to rattle off the seemingly never-ending list of problems associated with HIE. He explained the potential irreversible damage a severe lack of oxygen could cause and began to detail the life-changing therapy Sawyer was receiving. Since his arrival at Emory, Sawyer had been receiving cooling therapy. He lay on a special mat, lowering his internal body temperature to 92 degrees, where it would stay for a total of 72 hours. This therapy would give his body, brain, and internal organs the ability to slow down and attempt to heal themselves. His kidneys, which were previously showing signs of organ failure, were slowly beginning to function properly. The seizures he'd experienced directly after resuscitation had stopped, with medication, and we had high hopes that the cooling was working.

As the meeting went on, the amount of information that was flooding my brain began to feel like too much, and finally I began to crack. With my chest pounding with anxiety and tears in my voice, I mustered up the courage to ask out loud the scariest question of my life: "Will he make it?" At 21, almost 22, years of age, I sat in silent fear in a sterile, bleak back room of a hospital and asked a doctor I had just met what the chance of survival was for my child. I was 36 hours out of an emergency C-section, had been diagnosed with PTSD just that morning, and had been experiencing regular flashbacks to his birth. The words left my lips, and immediately I was terrified of what I had done. Did I want to know the answer? Was I even ready to hear it?

Without an ounce of hesitation, the doctor answered, "He *is* out of the woods." Overwhelming joy and the biggest sigh of relief overcame my whole being. A weight the size of a house lifted off my chest, and for the first time in days, I felt as if I could breathe. Anything else that was coming our way didn't matter; we could get through it. In that moment, the only thing that mattered was that he was out of the woods.

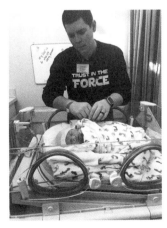

Sawyer remained on the cooling blanket for three days. For 72 full hours he lay there, wearing nothing but a diaper, as his internal body temperature remained a cool 92 degrees Fahrenheit. The time to rewarm him was quickly approaching, creating a new sense of panic in us all. We had made it this far; we couldn't go back now. Rewarming brought a whole new set of challenges, something that sent Zach and I both over the edge. In an attempt to calm us down and force us to rest, my mom volunteered herself to stay in the hospital, keeping a watchful eye on Sawyer as the rewarming took place and extended through the night. Thinking back on that night, she shared her experiences with me. From her reflection I wrote:

It was one of the most stressful nights of my life ever. Leading up to his rewarming, the doctors and nurses kept telling us the worst-case scenarios that could happen, and things to look out for. Thinking about being there, alone, for all of those worst-case scenarios was terrifying, but I knew Sara and Zach both did not need to be there. They desperately needed rest, so I volunteered to stay. Having lacked the ability to help so far, I was glad I could finally step up and do something. I was so thankful to be able to be there for them on such an important night. On the outside, I tried to keep my cool, to appear calm and collected, but internally, I was freaking out. The fear of the unknown married with the possibilities we faced during rewarming terrified me to my core.

I sat in the armchair in the corner of his room in the NICU, shifting back and forth as I tried to get comfortable. I was so tired, mentally and emotionally exhausted, while also doing my best to stay alert and awake. Due to the time cooling started on the night of his birth, they were not going to start warming him up until after midnight, after they reached the 72-hour mark. Time ticked on, the night getting later and later as I anxiously waited for the rewarming to begin. Despite my best efforts, I kept jerking myself awake, exhaustion taking over as I continued to fall asleep.

A gentle tap on the shoulder jolted me back awake, as one of the nurses had come in. Softly and kindly, she asked me if I wanted to go lay down in Sara's room to sleep for a while. With time still on the clock before the rewarming would began, I eagerly jumped at the opportunity. Sleepily, I followed as she took me through the hallways, back to the room the hospital was allowing Sara and Zach to stay in, and told me to try and get some sleep. She reassured me that she would personally come get me if anything with Sawyer changed or happened, and with that I knew I could rest.

I lay down, trying to get as comfortable as possible on the small, thin mattress, and attempted to get some sleep. I dozed off for a few minutes before going back into his room. My short nap gave me just enough energy to stay awake and keep an eye on Sawyer. Feeling refreshed, I began my journey back down the halls to Sawyer's room, arriving just after they started warming him.

I positioned myself back in my chair and settled in for one of the most stressful nights of my life. One of the side effects—we had been reminded time and time again—during the rewarming process was cardiac arrest. With this in mind, every time he would move or wiggle and a lead would unhook or pop off, I would freak out. With terror flowing through my body, each time I would jump up, run to his bedside, and check on him. Alarms seemed to go off nonstop, and once again all the worst-case scenarios ran rampant through my mind.

As time ticked on, I could see more pink flowing into his little body. With each passing moment, my grandson became more vibrant, looking physically better than the moment before. The physical transformation I witnessed was an amazing thing to experience. Reassurance of his success crept through my mind with each new sign of his recovery.

The morning after he was rewarmed and reached a regular tempera-
ture, I sat sleepily in the corner chair of the NICU, thankful that the night
was finally coming to a close. All of a sudden, I looked out the door of our
room and saw... Santa Claus? It was Santa Claus! One of the nurses I had
seen previously in the NICU was dressed in a bright red Santa suit. The
majority of the risks from the rewarming had passed, and seeing Santa
strolling through the NICU made it that much better. He walked around,
bouncing from one bed to another, a joyous smile upon his face. I sat up
tall in the chair, still in disbelief at the figure before me, and grinned ear
to ear as he turned the corner walked into Sawyer's room. The nurse had
confirmed just moments prior that Sawyer's rewarming was successful, and
now standing before me was Santa, ready to take a picture with him. I
quickly snapped a picture to send to Sara and Zach, attached alongside
the good news that Sawyer had been successfully rewarmed. After a night
filled with fear, anxiety, and unknowns, it was the perfect beacon of hope
and light shining through the darkness.

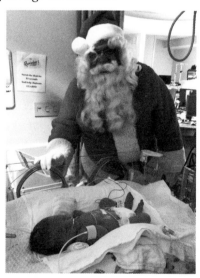

It had been four days since Sawyer was born, and I still hadn't held him. One by one we checked items off the list that were necessary before I could hold him in my arms. He had finished cooling therapy. *Check.* He had successfully been rewarmed. *Check.* His seizure medication had been altered, switched, and tweaked for optimum results. *Check.* He had successfully been taken off the ventilator and put on an oxygen cannula after rewarming. *Check.* He had gone through so much in his short time on earth, but today: Today was MRI day, the final item on the short, yet from our perspective extremely long, to-do list to be completed before we could hold him.

We had been anxiously awaiting this final step not only because it would lead to the much-awaited excitement of physically holding our baby, but also because it would tell us more about our son's life. An ultrasound of his brain had already confirmed no brain bleeds, but we still didn't have much information as to what damage his birth had actually caused. *Brain damage.* At four days of life, we were discussing the possibility of *life-altering* brain damage.

Twice over the course of that long-awaited Friday, the time for Sawyer's MRI was pushed back, making the already stressful day drag on and on. We were stuck between being thankful that his test was not as urgent as someone else's and being frustrated. Finally, it was time. As the team began to get him ready, Sawyer was placed into what I can only describe as a taco suit. He was all bundled up and ready to go. The distraction of how cute he looked wrapped up was the only way I was able to breathe as they prepared to walk out of the room. My tiny little seven-pound baby was wheeled out of the NICU by an entourage of nurses as they began their winding descent through the hospital to where he would get his test done.

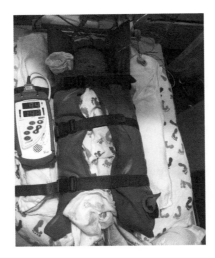

It was about an hour and a half before he would return to his room in the NICU, and to say those 90 minutes went by slowly would be an understatement. The weight that this test held was indescribable. My chest began to tighten, my palms began to sweat, and once again, my mind began to race with possibilities. Before, we could only think about the "what-ifs" of his diagnosis, but soon, we would know more. More about his brain injury. More about his potential quality of life. Zach and I carefully walked to the hospital cafeteria while we waited. We knew we wanted to stay close just in case something happened. In an attempt to pass the time, we choked down some food, barely even paying attention to what exactly we were eating.

We spent the majority of those 90 minutes in prayer. Huddled together in the atrium outside the hospital cafeteria, we bowed our heads and began to pray. Doctors, nurses, and other patients with their families loudly existed around us. The hustle and bustle of a busy hospital in the winter created a deafening atmosphere, yet we were unaware of the distractions surrounding us. We existed in a bubble of prayer, talking only to God, focusing only on Him as we came to Him yet again for our son.

After what seemed like a lifetime of waiting, we began our journey back upstairs to the NICU. We badged in, scrubbed and washed our hands, and walked down the hall to the "back room," the room where the sickest of babies were put. The room in which our son resided.

We walked in just moments before Sawyer's transfer team arrived. They greeted us with the pleasant smiles and the news that Sawyer was well-behaved and did amazing throughout the test. He did not need any medication and was still as could be (looking back now, that might have been the last time he was ever actually still). Because it was Friday, we were told that the team hoped to have his results read and transcribed by Monday.

Once again, we began the waiting game. As someone who struggles with patience, my skills were being tested more now than ever before. The *what-ifs* began to set in, and I now had an entire weekend to dwell on the hypothetical answers to these questions. What would the test results say? How would these results affect us? How would they affect him?

Before a million thoughts and fears could fully cloud my head, I was surprised with something that rid my brain of all the negative things. **I was able to hold him.** For the first. Time. *Ever.* Four days after he came barreling into this world, gracing us with his presence and simultaneously taking years off my life, I was *finally* able to hold my precious baby.

The nurses helped prepare him to be held. He had heart monitors, a pulse ox cuff, an oxygen cannula, a feeding tube—the list goes on and on. Holding him was not easy, but man oh man was it *worth it.* I excitedly got myself ready in the chair. Like a kid on Christmas morning, I watched with wonder in my eyes as the cords and wires were carefully wrapped, blankets were moved and gathered, and the nurses began to raise him up and bring him to me. Extending my arms in preparation, I finally experienced the first touch. Skin to skin.

The second he was handed to me, my eyes filled up with tears, and before long I was unable to hold them in. Tears escaped my eyes, ran down my cheeks, and splashed on his sweet head. My son, wires and all, was finally in my arms. I had waited a lifetime for this moment. Prior to his birth, I always imagined our first moment would be emotional; however, I could never have imagined this.

That night, I held him, and held him, and held him some more. I held him until I physically couldn't keep my eyes open or my head up. My arms were aching and numb. My elbow was sore from resting on the chair. I never wanted to put him down. The wires, the impending MRI results, the unknowns—nothing else in the entire world mattered. For the first time ever, I was holding my baby. My beautiful, wonderful, amazing baby. My gift from God. My miracle.

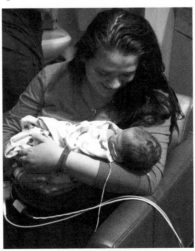

CHAPTER SIX
Turning a Corner

A fter the best weekend full of holding, cuddling, and loving on our boy, it was Monday. We had prayed all weekend for the results of the MRI, and finally it was here. All day long we knew that at any moment, the results could come back. Finally, around four o'clock in the afternoon, they arrived. *No significant damage indicated.*

Excitement met confusion met anxiety in that moment. None? Was the test wrong? Was there actually no damage or just none they could see? Would they have to redo the MRI, starting this whole process over again? It had been an entire week at this point since Sawyer was born. For *seven days* we were told to prepare for the worst, yet now we were being told that everything was . . . fine? How could this be possible!? Our son was born *dead*. Silent. Still. He was without oxygen for at least 20 minutes, possibly closer to 30, yet the MRI showed no signs of damage. The doctors seemed to have the same reaction we did. They were confused. They were excited. They felt the need to explain to us the effects that we could still be facing even with a clear scan. Cerebral palsy. ADHD. Learning disabilities. Seizures. Apnea. Little to no reflex response. A long list of maybes and what-ifs that were now being met with contradictory findings.

Over the next few days, Sawyer really began to turn a corner. Previously, he did not have the "suck, swallow, breathe" reflex, yet seemingly overnight, it appeared. He became more alert and stayed awake for longer periods of time. He showed no signs of seizure activity. He began to breathe more steadily on his own, until finally all oxygen help was taken away. One by one, wires were being removed, support being altered and then discontinued, and my baby looked less like a science experiment and more like my handsome little boy.

A few days after the MRI results, Zach and I got news that we needed to pack up the things in Sawyer's room because they were moving him. We knew we were nowhere near going home, so we began to wonder where he was going and why. Excitedly, the nurse assigned to Sawyer's care that day informed us that his status had been changed to stable. He was no longer critical, just a baby needing extra help to thrive. In an overwhelmingly excited rush, we quickly grabbed our belongings and started down the hall. Step by step, we followed as Sawyer's bed was wheeled away from the critical wing. The heavy double doors closed behind us, and for the first time since our arrival, we did not look back. The doors locking behind us created a sense of comfort and joy, and we continued to walk away, heads held high, knowing for the first time since his birth that we followed behind our son to bigger and better things.

Weaving through the halls of the NICU, we finally arrived at Sawyer's new home. No longer did he have a private room; this was instead a large, open space filled with babies, only separated by curtains hung from the ceiling. It was *perfect*. We quickly realized that Sawyer was not a fan of other babies crying, often making faces when he would hear one of his new roommates make a noise. His dad and I, however, longed for the day that we would hear those noises coming from our child. Through every obstacle we had overcome, we still had not heard our son make a noise. Day in and day out we longed to hear a cry, a grunt, a squeak come from his tiny body. We started to worry that maybe this was one of those complications the doctors warned us could still appear. For 15 days after his birth, our son was as silent as could be.

On December 20, my 22nd birthday, that all changed. Zach, along with both of our families and a few nurses, convinced me to leave the hospital and go out to dinner—somewhere other than the hospital cafeteria—to celebrate my birthday. Being in downtown Atlanta, we opted to go to the Hard Rock Cafe, and for the first time in 15 days, we truly enjoyed ourselves. We talked about how far Sawyer had come. We dreamed of the day he would come home with us. We discussed what Christmas would look like this year, and if we would still be in the hospital. We excitedly recollected Jessie's arrival from basic training earlier that day. For weeks we agonized over her arrival, planned out exactly how we would tell her what had happened since she called me while I was in labor, and looked forward to her finally being able to meet Sawyer for the first time. Seeing her the afternoon of my birthday, walking through the halls of the hospital, still in uniform, and filled with the emotions of Sawyer's birth gave Zach and I a new hope as we were able to hug her close while sharing positive news of Sawyer's miraculous improvements. As we headed back to the hospital, hand in hand, I began to feel the way I had longed to feel for so long. I felt like I belonged.

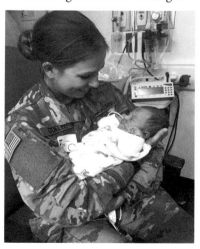

My husband and I had conversations that *normal* new parents have. We were excited to get back to see our baby instead of fearful for the news that we might be met with upon our return. We got back to the hospital and walked up to the NICU, and as Zach went to put our things down in our room, I headed to see Sawyer. Just like every day before, I went to his area, picked him up, and sat down to hold and snuggle him before bed. I talked to the nurses about our night, and then to the surprise of everyone in the room, we heard something new. Sawyer made a noise. For the first time in his entire life, he made the tiniest little noise. It was not a cry, or even a grunt, but the smallest, most perfect little wail. The most beautiful noise I had ever heard.

Instantly I began to cry. My heart burst with joy. A noise I was not sure I would ever hear washed over me, and for the rest of the night I basked in the joy that was the noise that came from his lips. I contentedly rested by his bedside, gently rocking him in the chair in his room, a memory forever ingrained in me. The best birthday present I had ever received. The best birthday I had ever had.

December 23 started out like every other day since our hospital stay began. Zach worked overnight, and when he arrived at the hospital in the morning, I was finishing pumping milk for Sawyer. We said good morning to each other, I cleaned the pump while he took off his gear, and as I began to leave toward Sawyer's room, he prepared to go to sleep. The single twin bed in our room almost always had somebody sleeping in it, as we all took turns resting, working, and spending time with Sawyer. I walked out of our room, beginning the journey I had taken so many times before. Out the doors of our room, I walked directly across the hall to the NICU entrance. I picked up the phone hanging on the wall and waited as it rang. The receptionist on the other end asked who I was there to see, and I repeated Sawyer's name back. There was a loud buzz followed by a click of the door as it unlocked. I was let in and started my way to the hand washing station. I turned the water on, pumped the antibacterial soap into my hands, and stared at the signs on the wall about proper hygiene and handwashing just like I had every day prior. This day was different though. I dried my hands, grabbed the milk I had just pumped, and rounded the corner into Sawyer's room.

"—Discharge." As I walked in, the doctors and nurses were all sitting at their stations in the middle of the room, and for the first time, I heard this magical word in reference to my child. "—Discharge—" There it was again. "Mrs. Schneider, do you want to join us for rounds this morning?" one of the doctors asked me. Hesitant yet excited, I pulled up a chair and sat down. "How do you feel about going home today?" they asked me.

Home!? *Today!?!?* I could not hold in my excitement as these words teased my ears. *"Yes!"* I squealed back. The idea of going home as a family of three seemed like a fairytale Zach and I had dreamt up, and yet here we were. I rushed back to the room where Zach was sleeping and began to shake him awake. *"We are going home . . . today!!"* I told him, barely holding back tears of excitement and relief. Finally, it was time.

Sawyer passed his car seat test, all the wires and tubes were removed, and we loaded our things up on a rolling cart, turned in our hospital badges, and began our grand exit—baby in hand. As soon as we were in our car, we began to giggle. This didn't feel real. As we exited the parking deck for the last time and started our long-awaited journey home, the reality of the day finally hit us. We were home free, and nothing could stop us now. A family finally reunited as one. We pulled into our driveway together for the first time since before Sawyer was born. The magic of being home after an extended time away felt even more special as this time, we were coming back with a new family member.

Walking in the front door, we saw a banner hung from the curtains in our living room saying "Welcome home, Sawyer." My littlest sister, too young at the time to visit at the NICU, stood with Jessie in the living room, anxiously ready to finally meet her nephew for the first time. These were the moments you prepare for when you're expecting a baby, and for the first time in 18 days, we got to experience them to the fullest. We held him, showed him around his new home, and began to truly settle into our life as a new family of three.

As I sat down on the couch to feed Sawyer, I began to think of my own birth story. I was an NICU baby myself, born in December, and after confirming with my mom, I realized I too came home on December 23. Two babies, mother and son, released from the NICU on the exact same day, 22 years apart. Gratitude washed over me. God knew what He was doing, and in that moment, we saw the beautiful tapestry He was weaving in our lives. We were home for Christmas, and although that Christmas was not filled with many presents under the tree or carefully planned and thought-out meals, it was spent surrounded by family. It was filled with more love, joy, and peace than any Christmas before it. The lights seemed to shine a little brighter. The music brought us to tears. The candlelight service at church was more special than ever before. We embodied the true meaning of the season that year. Our eyes were set firmly on God and His sacrifice. We praised Him endlessly.

Journaling has become therapeutic for me. Chaos constantly runs through my mind, and getting my thoughts out on paper helps to calm it all down. In a journal entry from those first few weeks home, I wrote:

It's 3:50 in the morning. I'm halfway through feeding and changing Sawyer after my alarm to take antibiotics for my incision woke us both up. So far, I have managed to go to the bathroom myself and take my pill all while feeding him. What else can I get done with my one available hand? I start to look around the room thinking of the other things I need to do before returning to sleep. Then, I look down at Sawyer. His beautiful blue eyes are wide open, and he's looking back at me. He doesn't know that it's almost 4 a.m. and I am beyond tired, yet I have no fresh breast milk left to give him and I must pump after this, prolonging once again when I can go back to sleep. He has no clue that once again, I had to bring him into the bathroom with me just because I had waited so long to take care of myself that I physically could not hold it in anymore. No. Instead, all he knows is my love. My service unto him. Because of me, he is fed. He is clean. He is happy. He looks at me and knows he is safe. He smells my scent and calms down. At only six and a half weeks old, he knows that I am comfort. I am safety. I am love.

I finish his feeding and lay him back down. How often do I take for granted these special moments with him? How often do I dread them? Waking up in the middle of the night to a tiny screaming infant is hard, I'm not going to lie, but as I am sitting here reflecting on my duties as his mother, I cannot help but feel blessed. Blessed to be chosen to be his mother. I'm grateful and thankful and overwhelmingly . . . blessed. God oftentimes shows Himself to me in ways I would never imagine, and this is no different. Just as Sawyer needs me, I need God. How often I have cried out to Him in the middle of the night, needing His encouragement, needing His love! He is my safety, my comfort. He is love. Just as I serve this sweet baby every hour of every day, I must also serve God.

It isn't always easy. If I am being completely honest, I have fallen off the path a few times in my life as well. However, each time I find my way, He is still there, waiting on my return. He is there, knowing that through Him I will find my way.

If I have learned one thing over the past six and a half weeks, it's this: Motherhood is hard. Physically, emotionally, mentally. It's hard looking in the mirror or stepping on the scale. So often, I find myself filled with frustration. I hate seeing stretch marks all over my body, and clothes not fitting like they used to. Sometimes all I want is to be able to put Sawyer down so I can get things done around the house or relax and take a minute to myself. But then I think about how God chose me *to carry my baby. And how God chose my body to house him for nine months and then to birth him and be his mommy. I wouldn't trade a single stretch mark or number on the scale, a single dirty dish or unwashed piece of laundry for anything if it meant not being able to be this sweet baby's mom.*

I think about how God chose me to witness His work firsthand through the miracle that is our son. He is allowing me to share this story and to be a witness unto Him through Sawyer. I know that 4 a.m. won't always be easy. In fact, I know there will be other times of the day that will sometimes be even more challenging, and that is okay with me. One look into those big blue eyes and I'm reminded how lucky I am. How blessed I am. How thankful I am for these moments.

Part Two

CHAPTER SEVEN
Waiting for the Other Shoe to Drop

S awyer seemed to be developing appropriately, but with every win there was a whisper in our ear telling us not to get too comfortable. Developmental delays could still appear through age five, a statistic that was drilled into our heads over and over again. We knew we wanted more children, and at every turn we were told that special needs children benefit from having siblings close in age to help their development. With these unknowns and statistics repeatedly entering our minds, Zach and I decided we wanted to give our boy a sibling sooner rather than later, and when Sawyer was only ten months old, we became pregnant with his brother. The excitement of our upcoming new addition made us giddy, knowing that soon we would have a new baby to love on. We planned Sawyer's first birthday party, an event we did not know if we would ever be able to celebrate just ten short months earlier, while holding the biggest secret close to our hearts. Family, friends, and hospital staff all gathered to celebrate Sawyer's birth and how far he had come. We felt as if we were finally living in our own personal fairytale.

We prepared to tell our families at Christmas, a holiday that had become so significant to us since just the year before, we finally brought Sawyer home in time for it. Ultrasounds showed a healthy baby growing in my tummy, pictures that we carefully packed and wrapped in boxes to be delivered as Christmas presents. They were elated, jumping for joy at the news that we would soon have another baby joining our family.

At 13 weeks pregnant, we found out we were having a second boy: an answered prayer once again. Sawyer would be receiving a little brother this summer, a built in best friend. We began to imagine all the trouble they would get into, thick as thieves. My pregnancy this time around was "textbook" healthy. My blood pressure remained perfect. My energy levels were high despite having a toddler at home, and I was able to be more active than before. Mentally, however, the closer we got to my due date, the more anxious I became. Would I hear my baby cry this time around? Would we have an NICU stay? The negatives were all I knew, and as much as I tried to focus on the positives, I kept falling back into a state of anxiety and fear. Each time I walked into the doctor's office, my heart began to race. I begged my doctor to take the baby early, regardless of medical need. The idea of going past 37 weeks and 3 days, the gestation Sawyer was born at, left me in a puddle. Despite my best efforts, I could not remain calm.

Zach was enrolled in the police academy, unable to take time off. I needed this baby to be born on a weekend. I needed Zach there with me. The idea of labor without him terrified me, and the lack of control continued to make me spiral. 35 weeks came, and I began to pray for high blood pressure. If my numbers could just increase, they'd induce me, I thought to myself. 36 weeks in, I prayed for early labor. I was willing to risk a short NICU stay for prematurity if it meant that everything else was okay. Much to my dismay, everything remained "perfect." At 36 weeks and 6 days, I began to let go of the idea that he would be born anytime soon. I had a repeat C-section scheduled for 39 weeks, and my doctor had agreed to see me at a more frequent rate to ease my concerns.

On July 6, 2018, Zach, Sawyer, and I went out to dinner with my dad. My mom and sister had gone to Virginia to visit family and were coming home that night. We left dinner and headed home for the evening. As we did every night that summer, we loaded up Sawyer in his stroller and began our route around the neighborhood. We were only three houses in when I began contracting. Having just finished dinner, and being in denial that labor would come anytime soon, I ignored it. We continued walking. Up and down the hills, around corners, stopping to talk to neighbors along the way; I confirmed that I was still pregnant more times than I could count. I have always been told that you will know when you are in labor. Well, apparently that is not the case for everyone. When we returned home from our walk, I told Zach I was having some really light cramps. I sat down on my exercise ball and began to bounce around with Sawyer. Walking hadn't helped, bouncing wasn't helping, and I began to think to myself that maybe this was something more.

Zach took Sawyer upstairs to bed while I texted my OBGYN, asking her what natural labor felt like. I told her I was having what I thought were very mild contractions, since they had been consistently four min- utes apart for the past two hours. I was embarrassed: This was my second baby, so certainly I should have known what contractions were by then. I don't know if it was the trauma from Sawyer's birth or the drastic difference between induced and natural labor, but I was in denial over the very thing I had been praying would happen for weeks now.

I called my mom, who had just arrived home moments earlier, telling her we were heading to the hospital. Still in denial, I told her we would probably be sent home but that we wanted to check everything out to be safe. A few minutes later, my dad arrived at our house to stay with Sawyer, and Zach and I hopped in the car to head to the hospital. Fully convinced I was not having a baby anytime soon, we left our house with no bags and no car seat, completely unprepared. Getting in the elevator, we pressed the button for the third floor. The doors opened at the entrance to Labor and Delivery, and I was taken back to triage and hooked up to the monitors. My doctor had called ahead to let them know I was coming and possibly in labor. We had only been at the hospital for a few minutes before it was confirmed that I was, in fact, in labor. My IV was started, I was prepped for a C-section, and I went over the pros and cons of vaginal birth after cesarean, or VBAC for short. This was it. I was admitted and taken to a labor room. Still very much in denial, I agreed to attempt a VBAC, with the sole condition that Pitocin would not, under any circumstance, be used.

For the next eight hours, I kept telling my husband I thought they were going to send us home. By this time, my mom had arrived at the hospital, I was in a gown, and my water had broken. I was not in pain, though. Labor was supposed to be painful. With Sawyer, I could not breathe, yet now I was walking around, bouncing on a birthing ball, and joking around with my mom. I even declined to sleep, knowing that as soon as I fell asleep, I would be awoken with the news that they were sending me home. The trauma of Sawyer's birth made me unable to accept my current circumstances. It wasn't until I was eight centimeters dilated that I began to realize this was it. I was *actually* in labor. I was having a baby, and I would be having him *soon*.

The pain, the anxiety, and the excitement all hit me at once, like a Mack truck coming at me at full force, as I finally accepted that I was transitioning from having one child to two. In my inability to accept my labor, I had waited too long to get a working epidural, and I was about to do this all-natural. Before I knew it, it was go time, again. Time to start pushing. The very moment where everything changed before. I started pushing, and almost instantly, my mind took me back to Sawyer's birth. A few days after Sawyer was born, I had received a PTSD diagnosis, and in that moment, I experienced one of the biggest episodes I had ever had before.

Where was I? What was happening? I began to gather my thoughts to the best of my ability. *I'm in labor. Oh no, labor. Sawyer. His heart rate, it's crashing. I can't breathe. Someone help me. Someone help him. My son is dying.*

Panicking, I began to hyperventilate. I did not know which baby this was. I did not know that Sawyer was okay. What was happening? I knew that I was in the hospital. I knew I was in labor. I knew in my soul that something was wrong. "Is he okay? Is his heart beating? How is his heart rate?" I frantically repeated over and over again. Brandy, my nurse through both Sawyer's birth and this birth, immediately jumped into action. Wasting no time at all, she took my legs out of the stirrups, quickly put the bed back together, and began to reassure me that everything was okay. In a gentle showing of love and respect, nurses began to rush the room—this time, however, for me. Helping me to breathe, calming my nerves, and stroking my arm, they fought to pull me back to reality.

Zach calmly yet firmly told me Sawyer was okay. He explained to me that he was safe, at home, and that this was a different baby. A different labor. My mom gripped my hand and, with her other hand, ran her fingers through my hair in an act of comfort. Our brains are a diverse, complicated muscle, and in that moment, mine was playing the biggest trick on me.

After what seemed like a lifetime, I finally began to realize that what Brandy, Zach, and my mom were saying to me was true. Sawyer was okay. This was a different baby. Slowly, I started to breathe again: shaky at first, smoothing out with each breath. Soon, I was back in the right headspace. We began again. *I can do this. I can do this.* I pushed for an hour with this baby, this new baby, this different baby, my focus now not only on my current physical hurdle, but the mental one as well.

CHAPTER EIGHT

A Miracle Born Again

"Open your eyes," I heard my doctor say. With the concentration and focus I had dedicated to both pushing and reminding myself where I was, I hadn't even realized he was born. Anxiously peeking through eyes squeezed nearly shut, I saw him for the first time. Dawson Barrett was born on July 7, 2018 at 11:15 a.m. Pink. He was *pink! My baby is* alive. *My baby is* breathing. *My baby is* crying!

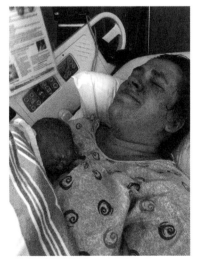

The nurses put him on my chest, and for a single moment in time, I was healed. Nothing else in the world mattered. That moment, however, did not last very long. Seemingly in the blink of an eye, my bubble of bliss shattered. Just as quickly as he was placed on my chest, he was whisked back away. From outward appearances, it seemed like he had swallowed too much fluid when he was born. Reassuring me that everything would soon be ok, the NICU team took him back down the hall I had traveled once before, beginning an attempt to suction out his lungs.

Confident and blissfully unaware, I sent Zach home to get the hospital bags we had left the night before, pick up the car seat, and return to spend time with our family. Too soon for him to be back, the door to my room opened again. A NICU nurse I recognized from Sawyer's birth walked in, a look I was no stranger to spread across her face. After taking Dawson to the NICU, they had discovered that he had not actually swallowed fluid, but instead a much more serious event had occurred. Upon entry to the NICU, all babies receive a chest x-ray, and thanks to this required exam, it was determined that upon his birth he had developed a pneumothorax. His left lung was deflated.

Defeat washed over me. Everything had gone according to plan. He was healthy, he was *crying*! My world came crashing down as the nurse explained to me more about what a pneumothorax is. As Dawson transitioned from the womb to the world, the pressure was too much for his small body, causing his lung to collapse. The NICU team tried needling the air out in an attempt to reinflate the lung, but they were unsuccessful. Instead, he required a surgical procedure. As the nurse was talking to me about his condition, a surgical team hovered over my tiny baby, inserting a tube into the side of his chest. This tube pulled any fluid and air out of his chest, allowing the lung to reinflate and heal. As the NICU team stood before me, telling me his prognosis and explaining to me what had happened, the world around me seemed to fade away. My thoughts began to run wild as I was overcome with emotion.

At first, I was in shock. *How could this be happening again?* I felt relief, because *at least he came out crying.* I was in denial that this meant another NICU stay. *Soon*, I thought, *the team would bring him back to my room; surely by the end of the day,* definitely *by our time to go home.* "There is a possibility we will have to transfer him to another hospital," I heard next. Reality hit me in the face, harder and faster than I could have ever prepared for. Transfer. Not again. *I can't do this again, please, do not take my baby.* Zach returned to the hospital, excited for the hospital experience we never received with Sawyer, only for me to tell him the news I was just delivered. As our worlds began crashing down once again, we began to pray. *Please, God, heal Dawson. Please, God, keep him here, don't take him to another hospital. Please, God, give us the strength to do this all over again.* Talks of transfer began to fill the air, and in the blink of an eye, Zach and I were right back to that December night. As anxiety took over, my doctor stepped in, a superhero in scrubs, and fought to keep Dawson with us. He was not being transferred due to the severity of his illness, but instead due to the number of babies in the NICU. Soon, we were given the news: He would stay. A wave of relief washed over us. Confidently, we knew we could do another NICU stay as long as he was here. With us. Together.

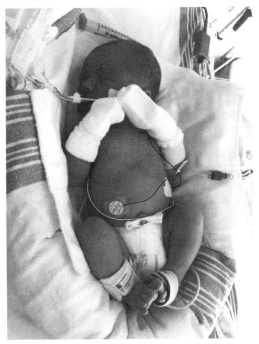

For the next six days, we visited Dawson in the NICU. Wires, phototherapy lights, and tubes draped across his small body. A tube remained in his side to repair his lung. A ventilator was in his mouth, keeping him alive. Stickers connected to wires were stuck on his chest to monitor his heart rate, and a pulse ox attached to his foot measured his oxygen. Deja vu. Between the ventilator and the chest tube, we were not able to hold him right away, and for the second time in my life, my arms felt empty. Nothingness remained where my baby should be. My heart longed to hold him, to kiss his head and cradle his body. I studied his features as best I could from his bedside, but my heart wanted so much more.

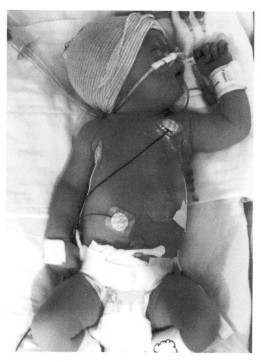

CHAPTER NINE

NICU Alumni

O ne by one, his monitors began to come off. First, the ventilator. He transitioned for some time to a nasal cannula to offer breathing assistance, before eventually we were able to see his beautiful face, free of obstruction. Second, the chest tube. A successful removal meant two healthy lungs. Major success. The light at the end of the tunnel began to illuminate, brightening the whole room. The removal of these two devices meant two things: One, we were one step closer to going home, and two, *I could hold him.*

The ability to hold, love on, and care for my son made the rest of the time in the NICU fly by. Day by day, we watched as Dawson grew stronger. His lungs were healthy, his bilirubin levels were normal, and he began to breathe entirely on his own. Finally, it was time: Time to go home. Time to introduce him to his big brother. Time to be united for the first time as a family of four. We packed up our room in the NICU and began the journey back toward the labor and delivery unit of the hospital and our grand exit. Waiting just outside the doors was a proud big brother. Only 19 months old, Sawyer was so excited for the baby he would soon get to meet. A moment I had dreamt of for the past nine months was finally here.

Robin, one of the nurses who played a major role in Sawyer's resuscitation, quickly exited the double doors, swooped Sawyer up into her arms, and walked back into the NICU with him. With Sawyer in her arms and Dawson in mine, the moment we had all been waiting for was finally here. The look of wonder on Sawyer's face as he finally got to see his baby brother in person is forever burned into my memory. Love, joy, and gratitude began to burst inside me; I was overwhelmed with the best emotions possible as I watched my two sons interact for the first time ever.

The past six days had not been easy. Navigating the NICU for the second time, this time with a 19-month-old at home and a husband in mandatory training, certainly had its challenges. Had it not been for our family, I do not know how we would have made it through. This moment, however, made it all worth it. Every back-and-forth trip. Every lunch box filled with snacks to keep me going, and every trip to the hospital cafeteria. Every pumping session by Dawson's bedside and every sleepless night led up to this moment, and with all that it brought me, I would not trade it for the world.

Dressed in matching "NICU graduate" and "NICU alumni" shirts, we departed the NICU for the second time, this time with *both* my boys by my side. We loaded up the car and drove home to start our new journey.

Zach's police academy enrollment added to the chaos of having a toddler and new baby at home. During Dawson's NICU stay, Zach had attended the academy during the day and spent the evenings at the hospital with us. On July 23, ten days after Dawson came home, my phone rang with a call from him in the middle of the day. I excitedly answered, exclaiming to him that for the first time ever, I had got both boys down to nap at the same time! My excitement was quickly muted by the tone of his voice on the other end. "I need you to come pick me up," he began. "I got hurt, I need to go to urgent care, and they aren't letting me drive." *What!?* Silence. For the first time in a long time, I was speechless. Hurt? How was he hurt? Was he okay? What did this mean about his progress in the academy? He was almost done! What was I supposed to do, I'd just gotten the babies down to nap! I took a deep breath and told him I'd be there soon before hanging up the phone and calling my parents.

I quickly pumped for Dawson, restocked the diapers and wipes downstairs, and got myself dressed as I waited for someone to come watch the boys. Seemingly in no time at all, my dad walked in the front door of my house, gave me a hug and a kiss on the forehead, and told me to breathe. He has always been the best at calming me down and centering me. He reassured me that the boys would be okay and told me to go take care of their daddy, and with that, off I went.

I was two weeks postpartum, with a 19-month-old, a newborn, and now an injured husband. Was this a joke? I drove to the academy, picked up Zach, and took him to urgent care. Torn rotator cuff. Possible surgery. Strict restrictions. No work. Defeat. My extremely hands-on husband was now not able to hold or carry either of our children, and had been medically removed from the academy. His dreams and spirit were crushed as we began to navigate his injury and healing.

In the month of July alone, our emotions had traveled the longest, windiest, craziest rollercoaster either of us had ever experienced. We were overjoyed at the new addition to our family. We had been anxious and stressed at a second NICU stay. We experienced excitement and antici-pation to be healthy and home from the hospital. We experienced defeat, fear, and heartache at his injury and medical discharge from the academy, and we were now left feeling as if life just wasn't fair.

CHAPTER TEN

Is This a Joke?

For the next six months, our family experienced so much pain, so many trials, and the biggest test of our faith since Sawyer's birth. Zach attended physical therapy two to three times a week for his shoulder, while working desk duty at the sheriff's office as he healed. The possibility of surgery had not been completely taken off the table, but had significantly lessened with the work he was putting in. Just when we thought we might be rounding a corner, it was my turn to fall ill. While I was standing in our living room one morning after Zach got home from working the night shift, the entire left side of my body went numb. I collapsed on the floor in front of him, completely unaware of what was happening.

Zach stayed home with our boys, Dawson being only four months old at the time, while my best friend, Kayla, rushed me to the hospital. I was admitted almost immediately, doctors and nurses rushing around hoping to find the cause of my collapse. Blood work, urine tests, and ultrasounds quickly were performed, and soon, a doctor walked into my room. The next words out of his mouth shocked me in a way I was not expecting.

"You're pregnant," he started. Cutting him off, I replied, "No, I'm not." Surely he was wrong, I thought to myself. Confusion spread across his face as he began again, "You're pregnant, and unfortunately, it is ectopic. The pregnancy is in your left fallopian tube. A doctor from the

OBGYN's office is on their way downstairs now to talk to you more and go over your options."

Frozen. *I-I-I-I'm* what!? Pregnant!? *No way!* We were **not** trying to have another baby, not right now at least. Kayla and I sat and stared at each other, processing the information we'd just received. "What do I do now!?"

Before either of us could even begin to answer that question, the OBGYN walked in the room. A doctor I had seen many times before, he was kind and gentle. "Pregnancy number three, right?" he began.

In that moment, it hit me. I was pregnant. For the third time. What was I going to do!? I had heard of ectopic pregnancies before but had never known anyone to have one. I honestly was not sure I fully understood what it meant to have one. "You have two options," he continued. "We can go right now into surgery and remove the left tube, or we can go an alternative route and administer methotrexate. This is a chemotherapy drug that will hopefully allow you to save your tube. There is a possibility that your tube could still rupture, that you will need emergency surgery, and you might end up needing a second dosage in a few days if your numbers are not where we want or need them to be." Information overload.

My eyes were wide, my heart was beating fast, and I had no idea what to say or do next. "Can I have some time to decide?" I asked him. "I can give you about ten minutes, but if we're going for surgery, we need to go now. The possibility of rupture is severe and can kill you."

Trembling, I unlocked my phone and called Zach. As soon as he answered, I began the same way the doctor did when he walked in the room, "I'm pregnant." Without a moment of hesitation, Zach responded identically to me, "No, you're not." I was having the same conversation again from the other side.

I began to explain the type of pregnancy. I told him it was not viable, and the baby would not survive no matter what. I explained to him that the possibility of something happening to me was extremely high and that I only had a few minutes to make a decision. A decision that would affect me for the rest of my life. Together, we decided to try the methotrexate. Zach's shoulder was still injured, making him unable to help much with the kids, and the idea of me recovering from surgery seemed impossible given our current circumstances at home. The doctor returned, and I informed him of our decision. Soon, the methotrexate was administered into my body, and we waited.

The probability of rupture was so high, I was advised not to exert myself much physically. I could no longer hold my boys, and I relied heavily on my friends, neighbors, and parents to take care of me and them. Every other day, I had to return to the hospital to get my blood drawn, and five days after the initial dosage, it was determined that I would need a second round of shots.

The pain brought on by my ectopic was excruciating. Cramps like I had never experienced radiated throughout my body while nausea carried me through each day. My heating pad was my best friend, and every day I prayed that my tube would not rupture. Every day I prayed that I would not die and leave my family without me.

The peak of my pain erupted on December 9, 2018. Kayla and my mom had stepped in and planned Sawyer's birthday party at our home, and as the day went on, I began to feel weaker and weaker. We had planned on going to a Christmas concert at church after everyone left that night, and as the rest of my family got ready, I retreated to my bedroom. Hiding my pain as best I could, I convinced everyone else to go and enjoy the concert, that I would stay home and rest. I told them I was just tired from the day and that I would be fine. I spent the rest of the night in the bathroom, folded over in the fetal position, with tears running down my face. I had begun to rupture, and I was too afraid to admit it to myself or anyone else. Throughout the night, I cried and prayed, prayed and cried, and slowly, as time went on, the pain began to ease.

The next morning, I had a doctor's appointment, like I did every other day. The doctor walked in, and I began to explain to him the pain I had experienced the night before. Quickly he grabbed a portable ultrasound machine and examined me. "You began to rupture and internally bleed. It seems as if your body began to resolve the issue though." Anxiety. I couldn't breathe. How was this happening!? It had been almost a month since I was initially sentenced with this pain. "I need my mom," I blurted out. Sitting in the parking lot with the boys outside was my mom. My rock. I called and told her I needed her to come in, and without questioning, she began to unload the boys, put the double stroller together, and make her way upstairs.

"You have a few options here," began the doctor once she arrived by my side. "We can either take you back to surgery now and remove the tube, we can admit you to the hospital and monitor you, or you can go home on strict resting orders and follow up in 24 hours with us." Confidently, I chose option three. We had confirmed that the internal bleeding had reabsorbed into my body and the rupture had seemed to resolve itself. For the first time in my life, I asked for something to ease my anxiety, filled my prescription, and went home to rest.

For the next ten days, I lay on my couch, praying for another day at home with my babies. Finally, on December 20, my 24th birthday, my labs hit zero, and I was released. I was in the clear and could put the tragedy of this loss behind me. Ecstatic, I rushed home and held my babies so tight. The loss of this pregnancy stung my heart, but knowing I could have left Sawyer and Dawson without a mother stung worse. The thought of leaving Zach behind broke me. I chose to focus on the things I had over the things I had lost, and for the most part, it worked. My mind seemed free from the trauma I had endured, and the heartache of my miscarriage was cleverly disguised by the relief of my clean bill of health.

CHAPTER ELEVEN

Fighting for Fertility

F ollowing methotrexate, you are medically advised to wait three to six months per dosage to try to get pregnant again. The thought of another ectopic pregnancy terrified both Zach and myself, and for the first year following our loss, we did everything in our power to prevent another pregnancy. Around the one-year anniversary of my ectopic, however, we began to talk about having another baby. We agreed that our family was not complete, and there was an obvious hole in our lives. Since the day Dawson was born, we knew he was our middle child, and after a long, stressful year, we decided we were finally ready to make that a reality. The leading factor causing ectopic pregnancies is a previous ectopic pregnancy, and with this in mind, we took a different approach to my fertility. I kept track of every day of my cycle, knowing that the day I got that positive test, I would need to be seen immediately to start tracking my numbers in hopes of catching another ectopic as soon as possible.

Month after month, we tracked. Every cycle day, every test. Month after month, each test came back negative. For six months we tried and prayed, prayed and tried, and each month, we were greeted with the same answer: not pregnant. We started to get discouraged, wondering why we would not get pregnant. I had two children. I had been pregnant three times! Why was this any different? My annual appointment with my

OBGYN was just around the corner, and we decided I would talk to her about our journey then.

I arrived eager and slightly nervous to the doctor's office. Given my previous history, we decided it would be best to go ahead and get an ultrasound to see what was going on. Laying on the ultrasound table, it dawned on me. "The last time I had one of these, it was to confirm my tube had begun to rupture," I told the ultrasound tech. With compassion in her voice, she confirmed she could see the scarring left on my tube from that evening. She asked how the boys were doing and finished her exam.

It was time to see my doctor, Dr. Barrett—Dawson's namesake. I knew she would tell me exactly what was going on, and that she would not hold back. When she entered my room, the first thing she did was she sit down on her stool and ask how I was doing. I began to explain to her how Zach and I had been trying to conceive again and kept coming up short. The look of displeasure on her face was stronger than I had seen before. "You have polycystic ovary syndrome and secondary infertility," she broke the news to me. *Are you kidding me!?* I stared blankly back at her, mouth agape; once again, I had been rendered speechless. *People get pregnant and have babies every day,* why *is this so hard for me!?* I began to think.

Together, we went over my options and started our plan for fertility treatments. Zach and I decided we would try anything up to IVF, but if it came down to it, we would stop trying there. Month after month, we tried other forms of fertility treatment. Month after month, I tracked every cramp, symptom, and cycle day. Intimacy was out the window, and left in its place was another chore, another item on a chart, another box waiting to be checked. Month after month, I travelled to the doctor to get my blood drawn, and month after month we received the same answer. Even with the fertility drugs, my body would not ovulate. My hormone levels at 24 years old were those of a woman who had already gone through menopause. Month after month, our hearts broke a little more with each negative test result.

Eventually, we maxed out on the drugs and had reached the point where it was IVF or nothing. Physically and mentally, we knew we needed a break. The pressure Zach and I had put on ourselves had gotten to be too much, and we had reached our breaking point. Instead, we chose to put the faith of our family entirely in God's hands, firmly trusting that if we were to have another baby, He would make a way. The pain we felt every month when I would start my period, however, did not go away. Some months, we would cry. Some months, we would scream, and sometimes we just felt numb. Months quickly turned into years, and with each passing moment, our hope was chipped away just a little more.

CHAPTER TWELVE

An Unmentioned Birthday

Our family had experienced a lot of life since that cold December night when Sawyer was first born. While we rejoiced at Sawyer's successful discharge from both neurology and the developmental progress clinic, we began to shift our focus to Dawson. At seven months old he was diagnosed with fourth nerve palsy, a condition where a muscle in your eye is paralyzed. This caused his eye to drift upward and gave him double vision. The double vision caused him to tilt his head to the side to see, resulting in torticollis, shortening and tightening the muscles in his neck. Consequently, he underwent two eye surgeries at one and two years old in an attempt to repair and resolve this condition.

Following Dawson's surgeries, Zach was finally able to go back and graduate from the police academy. Together, we sold our first home and built a brand new one, all while fighting the seemingly unwinnable and never enjoyable battle of infertility. Before we knew it, we were celebrating Sawyer's sixth birthday. The day of his party, we found ourselves surrounded by family and friends in the newly finished basement of our dream home, watching and laughing as kids and adults alike ran around in an all-out nerf war. Foam bullets soared through the air, darting across the room and bouncing off of targets. Laughter echoed off the walls, and childlike joy was felt by everyone in attendance.

After our party guests left, hundreds of foam bullets were picked up, and the day started to wind down, Zach and I sat back and reflected on all the things that brought us to this moment. Snuggled together on the couch, we began to talk about the day Sawyer was born, recounting the fear and terror that radiated through our bodies. We talked about his first birthday, a day we never knew we would experience, and how all the while we were secretly excited about Dawson growing in my tummy. We remembered his second birthday, how I was on bed rest for my ectopic pregnancy and he was still recovering from his torn rotator cuff surgery.

One by one, we recounted the birthdays leading us to this moment. In the quiet of the night, the lights from the Christmas tree gently illuminating our living room and the warmth of the fire roaring in the fireplace, Zach and I were hit with a realization neither of us anticipated. This was the first of Sawyer's birthdays we had not previously been "warned about." When he was born, we were educated on the possibilities of his injury. Doctors, nurses, therapists, and specialists all told us about things that might arise around his first birthday. They talked about his second, third, fourth, and fifth birthdays too. Physical delays. Mental delays. Academic delays. Each year held its own set of problems, *except this year.* For the first time since our son was born, we had nothing to look for. Nothing to anticipate or dissect. For the first time, we had a *normal* birthday. The realization brought with it a giant sense of relief, and for the first time in six years, a weight of anticipation lifted off our shoulders. We excitedly scurried up the stairs and into Sawyer's room, tiptoed in, and each gave him a tiny kiss on his head before getting on our knees and praying abundant amounts of thanks to God over our sweet boy, watching him as he slept peacefully in his room. Our hearts overflowed with gratitude for the miracle lying in front of us.

Part Three

CHAPTER THIRTEEN

Two Pink Lines

January 25, 2023, started out like any other day. It was my best friend's birthday, the kids were in school, and I had run to the grocery store to pick up a few things we needed at home. I was driving home from the store when both my phone and my watch buzzed. It was a notification from my period tracker app, something I'd used far too frequently since my ectopic pregnancy and beginning this fight with infertility. At the next red light, I glanced at my watch. "It's time to take a pregnancy test" flashed in hot pink across the screen. *It's time to see another negative,* I thought to myself as the light turned green. I had no idea that I was even late at this point, and after four-plus years of infertility, I knew the drill. I had taken so many negative pregnancy tests that it was just another routine thing for me to add to the day's to-do list. I got home, unloaded my car, and let the dogs inside. Skipping up the stairs to my bathroom, I squatted to the floor, opened the cabinet, and dug my way to the back, reaching for the stash of pregnancy tests I always had on hand.

Completely unfazed, I opened the test, peed in the little plastic cup I grabbed out of the kitchen, and stuck the stick inside. *Okay,* I thought, *I took it.* The familiarity of failure began to creep up my spine. *It's going to be negative, they always are,* I reminded myself. Without a second thought, I laid the test down on the edge of the bathroom counter and went about my business. I'd begun to gather laundry, picking up towels and cleaning my bathroom, when something caught my eye. Two pink lines.

That couldn't be right. *Two!?* Surely my eyes were playing tricks on me. Two pink lines could only mean one thing: another ectopic pregnancy. I was in complete shock, probably even a little bit of denial, and I immediately picked up my phone and dialed. "OBGYN's office, how may I help you?" the receptionist on the other end of the phone answered cheerfully. I told them exactly what had happened: about my positive test, my infertility, and my previous ectopic pregnancy. I hastily explained my concerns, anxieties, and fears, and an appointment was set for the following week. It wasn't until I began to enter in the information for my appointment into the joint calendar that my husband and I share that I realized I should probably *also* tell him what just happened.

"Call me!" I texted him before almost immediately hitting the Face-Time button beside his contact photo. A few seconds passed before his face appeared on my phone. He was sitting at his desk at work, completely oblivious to the news I was about to share. He asked if everything was okay, and without a word, I flipped the camera around and showed him the test. Two pink lines. Looks of surprise, joy, confusion, and anxiety spread across his face, matching exactly with how I was feeling inside. Complete shock rattled us both. We could not believe it. Overjoyed, I began to cry. As tears flowed from my eyes, I prayed, thanking God profusely. We had all but given up on the desire for another child. Just the night before, I was having a conversation with a friend's mom, sharing with her how I was finally content if we only had the two boys.

Nothing could bring me down! The fear began to leave my body, and in its place, a giddy excitement filled every inch of my being. I got off the phone with my husband and immediately called my sister Jessie, my mom, and my best friends. I could not get over the excitement. I knew it was early and that there were risks, but I was so excited that I did not care. I chose to celebrate this life no matter how short it might be from the very beginning, and knowing what I do now about this sweet baby's story, that is exactly what I should have done.

The next week both flew by and seemed to take forever. It was time. My first appointment. Confirmation. I was still in shock walking into the doctor's office that morning, convinced my eyes were playing tricks on me when I saw the tiny blip on the ultrasound machine. The pregnancy was in the right place. I exhaled just a little. Blood was drawn, and my next appointment was set for a week and a half later. This time, we saw a sac on the screen. No heartbeat yet, but everything seemed to be going according to plan. More blood was drawn, my hormone levels were checked, and another appointment was made. It wasn't until my third ultrasound, when I heard the heartbeat and really got to see that there was an actual human baby forming inside of me, that I started to grasp the concept and accept the fact that we were about to have another child. This was it. I was pregnant. Every negative test, every tear, and every failure led to this moment right here. Our third baby was on their way.

We had a secret, and keeping it from the boys was driving me crazy. I held onto something that would change our family forever. I wanted nothing more than to shout it out, tell them the news, and celebrate the fact that they were going to be big brothers. I searched the internet for announcement ideas and landed on t-shirts. "Big Brother Again" spread across one in big bold letters, while the second matched with the words "Big Brother Finally." The shirts came, doctor's appointments continued to go smoothly, and I entered into my second trimester. Finally, the day was here: the day we would tell them a new baby was coming. Gently, I wrapped each shirt, labeled the gifts, and placed them on the kitchen table.

We called Sawyer and Dawson into the kitchen and showed them their gifts. Wrapping paper began to fly in every direction as they ripped open the presents. Each boy pulled out his shirt and began to sound out the words. Slowly, you could see the wheels begin to turn in their heads. "Big," Dawson started. "Brother . . ." Sawyer continued. A lightbulb went off in his head. *"Big. Brother. Again!?"* he exclaimed. The news had not quite registered to Dawson yet as Sawyer began to bounce excitedly up and down. "Wait, you're going to have another baby?" Sawyer exclaimed, "Are you adopting one or having one?!" Dawson caught on, squealing, "A baby!? A new baby?? For us??" Both boys had been asking for another sibling for a few years, and were overcome with joy knowing a baby would soon be here. "The day finally came!" Sawyer said, before bowing his head, closing his eyes, and praying, "Thank you, God, for giving Mom a baby, amen."

As I was sitting at work one morning, my phone buzzed. Test results from the doctor's office had come through. Excitedly, I opened my phone, logged into my patient portal, and opened the results. My fingers swiped across my phone at lightning speed as I scrolled down to the bottom. There, I found the gender results. Boy. Another boy. *Three boys!* Giddy with excitement, I texted Zach and told him the good news. I have been asked a million times if I ever wanted a little girl, or if we would ever try to have a girl, but I have always known I was a boy mom. I knew in my heart that God had created me to raise a generation of God-fearing men in a lost world. I knew that these boys were made for a purpose bigger than I could ever understand, and seeing them grow up and carry that out each and every day has been the biggest blessing of my entire life.

My other best friend, Amber, found out she was pregnant with her third baby shortly after I did, and soon we found out we were both having boys. The excitement of having babies close together grew stronger every day. We were due two weeks apart, and we knew these boys would grow up to be best friends, just like their siblings already were. We planned matching Halloween costumes, sent each other silly themed onesies, and planned their lives as if they were twins. Together, we sat around thinking of baby names and how we would decorate their nurseries. We had known each other and been friends for over 22 years, but had never been closer than we were at that moment. We shared every tear, every worry, and every piece of excitement, and we dreamt of the day our babies would share them too.

CHAPTER FOURTEEN

Back on the Battlefield

When my 20-week appointment came, we were all so excited. My husband's grandfather had just passed away, and the entire family was going to my appointment before taking him to the airport to go to the funeral. Zach's bags were packed and loaded in the car, and off we went. Sawyer and Dawson were both so excited to see their baby brother on the ultrasound. Driving to the hospital, we eagerly took turns talking about the appointment, sharing how we could not wait to hang the ultrasound pictures up on the fridge, and dreaming about the future to come. The ultrasound seemed normal. We saw ten tiny toes and ten tiny fingers. We confirmed that we were having a third boy, and we watched as the tiny baby wiggled around on the TV screen hanging on the wall. Sawyer and Dawson beamed with pride throughout the entire scan. We all walked out of the ultrasound room completely oblivious that our world was about to change forever.

I had no idea that anything was wrong until the doctor walked into the room. "Things just got a lot more difficult," he said. Confused and naive, I asked if there was an emergency happening with another patient, thinking he had to step out and I would need to see another doctor or reschedule the rest of my appointment. The next words he spoke shook me to my core. "No, for you," he started. "You have what we call incompetent cervix." *Excuse me? I . . . what?* My heart began beating a little faster. The sound of my heartbeat rose up to my ears. A hot, prickly feeling began to wash over my body as he continued. He told me that I was already four centimeters dilated, and that the water sac protecting the baby and helping him grow was so far out that they couldn't even see the opening of my cervix. *Panic.* I lay on that bed in a state of pure shock, terror, and panic. *I can't breathe. This isn't real.* I did not know what to even think, much less what to do next; all I knew was that I needed to know how I could save my son. Again.

Before my brain could even begin to process what was going on, the back door to my exam room opened again. In walked Mindy, one of the office's ultrasound techs who I have been friends with for close to 15 years. She'd seen the results of my ultrasound come across her computer and knew the boys had come with me to the appointment that day. Immediately, she'd stopped what she was doing and woven her way through the office to my room. She quickly whispered, "I saw the scan," to me as she walked over to the boys. She grabbed them both by the hands and took them out of the room, knowing Zach and I needed to have space alone together to plan what was next.

As soon as the door closed behind Mindy, Sawyer, and Dawson, I picked up my phone. Fingers shaking, I unlocked the screen, clicked on the call log, and tapped my mom's picture. A few rings passed before she picked up. As soon as I heard her voice, tears began to fall. "We might lose him," I choked out. "Something is wrong. I might not be able to carry him to term. We might lose him."

"I'm on my way," she replied, her voice shaky with fear and pain. As I hung up with Mom, I looked to Zach. He had called his parents. "I won't be making it to the funeral. Something is wrong, and we might lose the baby. I'll keep you updated as we know more," he told them. As soon as he hung up, he canceled his flight, and we started to look toward the next few actions we would take.

"We have a few options," the doctor began again once we got our bearings. "You could go home and wait, but given the scan, know that your water could break at any moment. You are not yet viable, so if that happens and you deliver, there is nothing we can do." *Okay, option one sucks, next.* "You do have the option to medically abort," he continued. *Absolutely not. Never. Next.* "Option three is both the riskiest and the least likely option for success," he went on. *Okay, I'm listening.* "With this option, we can take you directly to labor and delivery and put your feet over your head"—*so far so good, go on*—"and pray that gravity takes over, allowing your water sac to go back up where it belongs. *If* this happens, you could hopefully receive an emergency cerclage surgery to stitch your cervix closed. There is a possibility that we do all of this and your water still breaks, the inversion doesn't work, and you are not eligible for the surgery. There is also a high risk of infection, not only for the baby but for you as well," the doctor finished. Without a second thought, I confidently blurted out, "Option three."

I immediately knew that there was no other choice for me personally than to fight with everything I had for my son. Zach agreed. "I will tell you, looking at the scan, if this was a question on a test, I would confidently tell you that it will not work, but I am more than happy to try," the doctor informed us as he notified a nurse to get me a wheelchair. That was all I needed, a possibility to try, the ability to fight. I had never backed down from a fight before, and I was not about to start now.

Almost immediately, the wheelchair showed up at my door. Carefully, I climbed down from the exam table and lowered myself into the seat. We began our journey through the maze of halls leading back to Labor and Delivery. The first person I saw as I was wheeled through the double doors was Brandy. She had been with me through both Sawyer and Dawson's births, and in true Brandy fashion, she would not leave me now. She hugged me, let me cry on her shoulder, and stroked my hair as a different team of nurses prepared my room. Within a few minutes I was in a gown, up on the hospital bed, and inverted. For the next 31.5 hours, I lay there uncomfortably, my feet higher than my head, praying that this risk would pay off. Praying I would be a candidate for this surgery. Given the severity of my condition, the surgery didn't have very high projected success rates, but I needed to know that there was an option.

Finally, at five o'clock on Friday night, the surgeon came in, scanned me, and told me that if I still wanted to, he would be willing to attempt the surgery. "There are risks," he told me, rattling off the risks we had discussed two days prior. There was a risk that my water would break during the surgery. There was a risk of infection. There was a risk that it would not work. There was a risk we would lose the baby. Despite all the risks, I knew we had to try. I knew this was the best option we had to save him.

For the second time in my life, I lay back on a hospital bed as nurses and doctors wheeled me back to the operating room. Hospital lights once again passed by overhead as I began to prepare myself for another emergency surgery, my second emergency surgery in an attempt to save one of my unborn sons. We arrived in the operating room, which was much calmer than when I had my C-section with Sawyer, and began the emergency cerclage surgery. I prayed throughout it, remembering the peace I felt during Sawyer's birth and choosing to once again put my full trust in God. Before I knew it, it was over. The surgery was a success. *Thank you, Jesus.* I was taken back to my room to tell Zach the good news. The hospital monitored me over the weekend to ensure no infection began, and on Sunday morning I was discharged and sent home to rest. The team was hopeful I would make it the entire remainder of my pregnancy.

Wednesday morning, May 24, I got up at four o'clock to go to the bathroom. I was sleepily shuffling my way back to bed when I felt a pop followed by a gush. My water had broken. *No, no,* no. I knew in my heart what it was, but panic, denial, fear, and anxiety set in and took over. *This can't be happening. I had emergency surgery. Everything was okay. The surgery was successful.* Quickly, I grabbed a pillow, lay down on the floor, and put my hips up. Shaking, I started to pray, repeating over and over prayers that I had just peed on myself. I knew I had just gone to the bathroom. I knew exactly what it was, but I could not admit it to myself. Admitting it made it real.

I knew Zach would be waking up for work soon, so I decided to text him and tell him to come see me. I was sleeping in the downstairs guest room in an effort to be extra careful, and needed to tell him what had happened. By the time he walked in the room, full denial had taken over. I had completely convinced myself that I had just peed on myself again. I reminded myself over and over that I had the cerclage, that we had made it out of the woods. With that, I sent him to work. I already had an appointment later that afternoon, and I was convinced that everything would be okay.

The entire day I lay in bed, afraid to move. I prayed, I cried, and I did my best to distract myself. Finally, it was time for my appointment. Zach came home early from work, helped me into the car, and drove me to the hospital. During my ultrasound, it was confirmed that my water had broken, and once again, I was taken to Labor and Delivery, where I would remain until the baby was born.

The minimum age of viability for an unborn baby is 22 weeks. I arrived in shambles at Labor and Delivery at 21 weeks and 4 days pregnant. Shaking. Terrified. Defeated. Statistically speaking, most women go into labor within 24 hours of their water breaking, and my clock had been ticking for almost 12 hours already. After your water breaks, there is a high risk of infection, both for the baby and the mother. In these instances, the only possible solution is to deliver the baby. The odds were stacked against us. I prayed hard that I would be an outlier. I prayed hard that both the baby and I would be okay. Zach and I knew the chances of a viable delivery, and quickly agreed that *if* I made it to 22 weeks, I would be transferred by ambulance to a hospital with a higher-level NICU, a NICU that was better prepared to care for 22-week micro-preemies.

Every moment of every day, I tried to distract myself, praying that I would make it another 24 hours. Each second that ticked by was another moment closer to viability. Finally, Saturday came. I'd made it. I was 22 weeks pregnant. The day dragged on as I waited to be transferred. After what seemed like a lifetime, the EMTs walked into my room. They loaded me onto a gurney and strapped me in. I was loaded onto the ambulance, and off we went to the bigger hospital. The higher level NICU. Another hospital room. Another waiting game, yet one step closer to a safe, successful, live delivery.

Living in a hospital, I could not see Sawyer or Dawson like I normally would. Laying in a hospital bed, praying their brother would make it another day, my heart ached knowing I was without my boys. I had quickly learned that parenting from a hospital bed is nearly impossible. Since the cerclage surgery, my mom and dad had stepped in and taken over the responsibility of parenting for us. Zach lived at the hospital with me. He worked during the days before returning to the hospital to be with me during the evenings and nights. We did not know how long I would be in the hospital, or the length of NICU stay we faced once the baby arrived, and we wanted to be as prepared as possible. I spent a lot of time praying, thinking, and distracting myself with every possible opportunity. "One more day," I told myself every morning when I woke up and every night before bed, physically crossing days off the calendar my mom brought me. I watched a lot of Game Show Network, completed more crossword puzzles and word-searches than I ever had in my life, and spent an unbearable amount of time aimlessly scrolling through social media. We decorated my hospital room with Bible verses, inspirational signs, and family pictures.

My favorite parts of the day were when people would come to visit me, and I looked forward to sitting and talking. Friends, family, and neighbors delivered food to the hospital. Church members and coworkers delivered care packages. Our best friends planned a double-date night for the four of us in my hospital room. Each day, I would FaceTime with Sawyer and Dawson, counting down until I got to see them again. Day after day, I lay in my hospital bed, waiting and praying. I gave a lot of blood, answered countless questions, and prayed: that infection would hold off, that labor would hold off, and that my sweet baby boy would continue to grow big and strong inside of my body, knowing he was safe.

CHAPTER FIFTEEN

Tiny Fighter

June 8, 2023. After an uncomfortable night of sleep, I woke up feeling crampy. My water had broken 15 days previous. I had been on bed rest for 22 days. My back ached. My hips felt tight and weak. My shoulders and neck were stiff from the endless laying around. In an attempt to get more comfortable, I shifted from my hospital bed to one of the recliners in my room. I tried to eat breakfast, and after a few minutes, I decided I would rather be safe than sorry. Getting up, I grabbed the remote and called my nurse back to my room. "I'm still feeling crampy," I shared with her when she arrived. "Can you just ease my mind and check to make sure everything is okay?" Without hesitation, she hooked me back up to the monitors I had worn so many times before. This time was different, though. I was having contractions. I was in labor.

More nurses flooded into my room. With every contraction, they lost the baby's heart rate. It had previously been hard for them to find because he was so small. It could've been the way that he was positioned. They continued to search. The doctor was the next person to walk into my room. I knew once I saw him that something was really happening. Nurses continued to hold the monitors on my belly. I rolled from side to side as they watched the screen. "Where is your husband?" someone asked me. "Is he here with you?" "He's at work, should I call him?" I asked. "I would," they responded.

I still was not entirely sure what was going on, but quickly grabbed my phone and sent out a text. I told Zach he needed to leave work and come join me at the hospital. The scanning, flipping, and watching continued. Still no reply from Zach. The nurses' demeanor shifted from concerned to serious as the doctor returned to the room. "Is your husband on the way?" he asked. I told him Zach had not replied, and he told me to call. Without hesitation, I clicked call on his contact. After two rings, Zach picked up. "You need to come now," I said firmly. "On my way," he replied. Click. Call over. "He's coming," I told the doctor.

"With each contraction, we seem to be losing the baby's heart rate," the doctor told me. "We don't know where these contractions came from, or why they are so strong out of nowhere, but at this point it is more dangerous for the baby to be inside of your body. We need to get him out. We need to go now for an emergency C-section."

Immediately I went into fight-or-flight mode. I had traveled this road before, and knew what was coming next. Nurses worked quickly to strip me down and drape a gown over my body. As we wheeled out of the room, a nurse walked beside me, starting a new IV in my arm. For the third time in my life, I watched as hospital lights passed by overhead, trusting God and the medical staff beside me as I was wheeled into an operating room. Sitting on the table, it finally hit me. I was about to have a C-section. I was about to give birth. I was *alone*. The one thing I did not want was to be alone, again. I needed Zach. *Please get here. Hurry. Please.*

The team was moving so quickly around me that I did not have time to fully panic. The anesthesiologist performed my spinal block at lightning speed. One minute I was sitting up on the bed, and the next I was flung backwards, once again staring at the bright surgical lights overhead. Karen, the hospital chaplain, walked into the room right before the surgery started, and although Zach still had not arrived, I knew I was not alone. She was already on her way to check on me when she heard that I was being rushed to the operating room. A true angel sent from God: Having her by my side meant more to me than she will ever know.

A nurse appeared overhead, my phone in her hand. "Are you okay with me taking pictures for you? I want you to have pictures of his birth, especially with the chance that he does not make it out of the operating room," she asked gently, with genuine love and comfort in her voice. Without hesitation, I answered, "Absolutely. Please. Yes!" *Breathe.* Everything is okay. *Pray.* God's got this. *Breathe.* He is going to make it. *Pray.* Please, God, let him make it.

He's here. On June 8, 2023, at 8:41 a.m., Bowen Walker was born. Born almost 17 weeks early, at 23 weeks and 5 days gestation.

The NICU team was prepared and ready, jumping right into action for my boy. As time ticked on, Karen and I held hands, praying with confidence for Bowen's life. He had a heartbeat, and I prayed he would keep it. I'd done the best I could do for him, and now I had to trust the doctors and nurses to do their part. "Ventilator placed," we heard. Karen walked to the other side of the room to confirm before returning to me. "They were able to place him on the ventilator. He's alive. They're going to take him to the NICU." *Thank you, Jesus.* My whole body began to shake as I truly exhaled for the first time since calling my nurse in that morning. *He's alive. He survived birth.*

Karen had my phone now, the screen lit up, and for the first time I was able to see Bowen. He was so tiny. So beautiful. He weighed one pound and seven ounces, and was eleven and a half inches long. He was absolutely perfect, with ten little fingers, ten tiny toes, and the biggest personality I had ever seen. He was roughly the size of an action figure, and immediately he became my favorite superhero.

"Is there anyone I can call?" she asked. My mind started racing a million miles a minute. Nobody knew I had gone into labor, much less given birth. "My mom," I replied, "I need to tell my mom." I knew Zach would be arriving any minute now, and I needed to talk to the next most important person.

"Hello?" my mom answered. "Hey. Am I on speakerphone?" I asked. I could hear Sawyer and Dawson playing in the background and did not want them to know about the birth of their brother just yet. My mom took me off speakerphone before I started again: "Bowen is here. He's alive. I had an emergency C-section and am currently laying on the operating room table while they sew me back together. Zach is on his way and should be here any minute. I went into labor fast and furious, and we needed Bowen to come out to try and save his life. He is in the NICU now. I'll keep you updated. I love you." *Silence.* I could almost hear the wheels spinning in my mom's head as she began to digest what I had just told her. "Uhhh . . ." she began in an attempt to make sense of this new information, ". . . okay then. Wow. Okay. That was fast. I was just talking to you earlier and you were fine! I'm glad you're both okay. I love you!" I was hanging up the phone, still processing what had happened myself, when I looked over and saw Zach.

By the time he had arrived, Bowen was already in the NICU. We had not spoken since I called to tell him to come to the hospital. He had no idea I was in labor or that his son had already been born. It was not until he arrived at the hospital that he started to piece everything together. He arrived at the security desk to check in, giving the clerk my name. "Okay, one moment, she's in operating room two," she told him. "I'll take you back there now." The panic of the unknown set in as he began the journey back to the operating room. Quickly, he put on the scrubs he had been handed and walked through the double doors to me.

I looked to the door, locking eyes with him. He had the biggest smile on his face. "I'm so proud of you," he said as he walked to my side. Bowen was gone from the room, he'd missed the birth, and he had no idea whether his son was alive or not, yet the first thing out of his mouth was an act of love: *I'm so proud of you.* I still replay those words over and over in my head. I always knew I had married the right person, and that one moment confirmed it more than ever before. I could not imagine going through what we have gone through with anybody but him. God truly created him for me and me for him.

While the surgery team worked to finish closing my C-section and remove the cerclage, Karen and Zach ventured down to the NICU. They found where Bowen would be living for the foreseeable future and were able to ask when we would be able to go down and see him. We met again in Recovery, and Zach and I began to share the news of Bowen's arrival. We called our close friends and family, sharing his birth and asking for prayers. We knew Bowen was not anywhere close to being out of the woods, and that this was just the beginning of a long, hard battle. Together, we basked in the arrival of our third son, deciding to wait to tell Sawyer and Dawson until we had been allowed down in the NICU to see him ourselves.

"Would you like to take a trip down to the NICU before moving to your postpartum room?" the nurse in Recovery asked us. Zach and I both beamed with excitement as he nodded yes. Still laying on the hospital bed, I was wheeled down the hall, into an elevator, and down to the floor the NICU was on. We maneuvered our way into the room, and for the first time, Zach and I were able to gaze upon our newborn son. We met the NICU staff, briefly talked about what to expect during his stay, and took our first family picture. Before we left, Bowen's nurse handed me the tiniest diaper. At the top, where the size number usually is, were the letters "NP." Nano-preemie. The size of a car key-fob, it is the tiniest diaper they make—the size Bowen was currently wearing, yet still too big for his tiny body. I clutched the diaper close to my chest as I was wheeled out of the room, up the elevator, and down the hall to my new room.

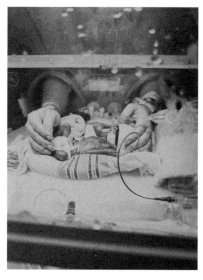

You would think that for three-time NICU parents, things would get easier. For us, it seemed to have the opposite effect. Instead of the process becoming easier, Zach and I struggled with reliving our past. We struggled with false hope as well as a lack of hope. It's a really weird experience to feel both hopeful and hopeless at the same time. We sat in my postpartum room, basking in the emotions of the day. *I really just had a baby. We really have three kids.*

After a few hours, we decided it was time to tell the boys. I found my mom's contact in my phone and tapped the FaceTime button. My mom answered almost immediately, and knowing the conversation we were about to have, she called the boys to the room. Sawyer and Dawson appeared on the phone, excited to see us on the other side. "You have a baby brother!" I told them. The sentiment behind my declaration did not immediately resonate, and Sawyer responded, "Mom, you already told us that. . . ." Grinning at his innocence and confusion, we explained further. "Bowen was born this morning. Today is his birthday!" Pure joy erupted from the other end of the phone. The excitement of their brother's birth made every moment of panic worth it. We explained that, although they were not allowed down in the NICU to see him, we could go to his room and FaceTime them as much as possible. We wanted them to feel included, and to get to know Bowen as much as they possibly could from afar. They were so intrigued by him, so in love, marveling over his tiny body and even smaller features. As they studied their little brother, pride beamed brightly from them both.

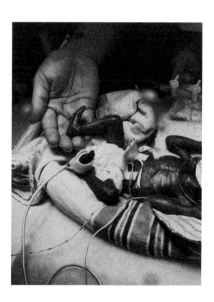

CHAPTER SIXTEEN

Down but Not Out

We saw God every single day in that NICU room. Bowen fought harder than anyone I've ever seen fight before, a giant personality flowing out of his tiny body. We had surpassed the 12-hour mark, blown through the 24-hour mark, and were beginning to see sunshine through the dark clouds of his early birth. The day after he was born, I was sitting in my hospital room, waiting on my nurse to help wheel me down to the NICU, when my phone began to ring. The NICU was calling me. Bowen had developed a pneumothorax in his right lung. Just like Dawson's, his lung had collapsed, and he needed a chest tube placed to reinflate it. The surgery went smoothly, and within the hour I was down in the NICU with my boy. It was a speed bump we had prepared for the possibility of, and we continued on our journey. We had entered the honeymoon phase of his birth, living in a bubble of bliss. His labs were improving. His organs began to function properly, and the ultrasound of his brain returned with beautiful results. A blip so small they could not confidently classify it as a brain bleed was present, and we were hopeful it would resolve on its own.

"Mom, do you want to change his diaper?" Bowen's nurse asked me. He was one day old and for the first time ever, I was able to *touch* him! I was not even able to change Sawyer or Dawson's diapers this early. The idea of touching something so small and fragile terrified me, while the prospect of feeling my son's skin against mine energized my soul. With uneasy confidence, scared to do anything wrong, I washed my hands, opened the window to his bed, and slid my arms inside. My first diaper change. I gently rubbed my finger against his soft skin as the nurse took his vitals, then assisted in changing the tiniest diaper ever. Everything on him was on such a small scale that flashbacks of my childhood began to flood my mind, memories of my sister and I dressing our Barbies. I rode the high of my first hands-on experience for the remainder of the day.

Day three started with a leak in his chest tube. His pulse ox monitor began to drop again, sounding off alarms when his doctor walked into the room. She was confident in the issue, and pressed her finger up against his side where the tube was placed. Immediately, his numbers began to improve, and the decision was made to replace the tube with a new one. After the replacement tube was placed, Zach and I sat down with the neonatologist to discuss Bowen's care. "The next few weeks will be a living hell," the doctor warned us. We discussed the weakness of his lungs, the underdevelopment of his gut, and the possibility of infections and brain bleeds. We had discussed our game plan, gathered our weapons, and dressed ourselves in armor. Zach and I were prepared to go to war for our boy, knowing we had the best team of doctors fighting right alongside us.

If you have ever spent time in the NICU, you know all too well the quiet ambience that is intertwined with frantic, never-ending stress: a battleground of warriors leaping to action surrounded by comforting voices, cartoon drawings, and tiny patients. As a NICU parent, you know how it feels to want to help in any way possible while also feeling more helpless than you ever have in your entire life. You struggle with the desire to do everything for your baby while knowing you are the most unqualified person in that room. I was always eager to change his diaper or take his temperature, jumping at the opportunity to help in any way possible. Every opportunity I was given to get my hands on him, I would. I would hold his finger every moment of every day, if I was allowed.

I clung to the words of Romans 12:12: "Rejoice in hope, be patient in tribulation, be constant in prayer" (ESV). Bowen continued to show improvement with each passing day. Each concern we discussed with the neonatologist seemed to be resolving itself, and we knew God was at work. His lungs looked to be improving. His gut finally started to move. He started tube feeds. Sawyer and Dawson were able to visit their brother from outside his window, seeing him in person for the first time. We existed in a bubble, and for the first time since my appointment on May 18, I felt truly happy. I felt as if everything would actually be okay. We knew we were not out of the woods yet, but we continued to take long strides in the right direction.

The pain of my C-section had really begun to set in, but watching Bowen fight gave me the strength to keep going. I spent as much time as possible in Bowen's room, taking breaks to rest upstairs. Each time we came back down to the NICU, we were met with new improvements. Suction for his chest tube was turned off, his oscillator settings had been adjusted and decreased, and his blood work showed that his body was successfully fighting off infection. *We will be okay. He will be okay. God is here with us. He's got this.* The only thing that could dampen my mood was the inevitable, something I had pushed out of my mind since the moment Bowen was born: discharge.

For the first time in almost a month, I was being sent home. Home, where two of my three boys were. Home, where my tiniest, sickest, most fragile son was not. Home, 45 minutes away from Bowen. For the third time in my life, I was leaving the hospital without my baby. Zach packed the car with a month's worth of personal items while I went over my discharge instructions and signed the paperwork, and then I slowly began my descent from my room. I was not ready, physically, mentally, or emotionally. *How was I expected to walk away from someone I had fought so hard for? Someone I prayed fervently for throughout the past four and a half years?*

Zach and I met at the elevator door and began our journey downstairs to see Bowen again, for the last time that night. With our arms draped around each other, and our free hands cradling the side of his bed, we bowed our heads and prayed over Bowen. We prayed for his health. We prayed for his safety. We prayed for the both of us as we journeyed home for the first time together without him. We told Bowen we loved him, and turned to walk back down the hall. My feet felt heavier with each step. *I can do this,* I reminded myself. "He will be okay," I whispered as I squeezed Zach's hand a little tighter. *One more step. One more inch. I can do this.* We had finally reached the NICU security desk and turned towards the elevator when I broke down. The pain overcame me, my heart ripped from my body, and I fell into the wall, tears streaming down my face. "I can't do this. I can't leave him," I repeated to Zach. The entire drive home, I cried, each mile feeling heavier than the last.

I spent my first night back home showered in love and affection from Sawyer and Dawson. With these two mama's boys glued to my side, I experienced a sense of normalcy for the first time in way too long. Waking up the next morning, I was eager, recharged, and ready to see my boy. A few days had passed since he initially got his chest tube, and if everything went well through the night, we would be removing it today. Still moving slow from my surgery, I carefully got dressed, packed a bag full of snacks and things to keep myself entertained, and climbed into my mom's car like a kid on Christmas, ready to begin my journey back to the NICU. I arrived right after the team had removed his chest tube, and excitedly jumped right in to help with hands-on care. We were finishing up in his bed when alarms in his room started going off, monitors beeping in a panic-inducing fashion. I froze in terror as Bowen began to code.

Overcome with fear, I watched his numbers drop one by one. I stood helplessly as doctors, nurses, respiratory therapists, and an x-ray tech all rushed into his room, before being shuffled into a corner. Trapped.

I began to shake as I watched other people work on my son. My heart felt like it was outside of my body. I felt so cold. Shivering, teeth-chattering cold. I began to pray. I have never wanted to be both present and anywhere else like I did in this moment. As a mom, I often struggle with the inability to be in two places at once, but in this moment I truly felt as if I needed and wanted to be in two completely separate places. On one hand, I could not leave his side. On the other hand, I was terrified to be in that room. There was nothing I could physically do to be helpful. All I could do was sit, watch, and pray.

After a few minutes, staff helped me out of the room as the x-ray machine was wheeled in. Almost immediately, we had the results. Another pneumothorax, less than an hour after the successful removal of his chest tube. Immediate defeat. It felt like we had taken one big step forward just to slide two bigger steps back. He needed another new chest tube. I sat in the waiting room, fear beginning to take over as I continued to replay the panic that had just erupted in his room. *This is not how I envisioned today going.* Over an hour passed before I was let back into his room—another successful chest tube placed. His will to live was astounding. After checking to make sure he was okay, Bowen's nurse lovingly convinced me to take some time for myself to breathe. I wearily made my way down the hall to the hospital cafeteria. Sitting alone, I tried to force myself to eat. *I am exclusively pumping for Bowen, I need to eat. I can't do much for him right now, but I can do this.*

Tears began to trickle down my face, and before I knew it, I had transitioned into a full-blown sob. Unable to control the tears as they poured out, I began helplessly crying out to God for help. Just as the words left my lips, a sweet older gentleman walked by my table. He paused, looking at me crying, and gently asked if I was okay. In a moment of vulnerability, I couldn't even begin to pretend that I was, and honestly told him no between cries. He walked over to me and asked about my tears. Taking a big breath, I began to share with him about Bowen. I told him about his birth, how small he was, and that he was not doing good. In that moment, in a crowded, loud hospital cafeteria, this sweet man, a stranger I had met just moments before, grabbed me by the hand and asked if he could pray for me. God heard my cries and sent this man to me. In my moment of weakness, I was reminded that He is near.

In that cafeteria, in the middle of the day, I sat and prayed with my new friend. My tears began to dry, and I started to see a new hope, a new light in my day. We sat and talked about why he was in the hospital, and he shared who he was there visiting before giving one another a big hug and departing. I finished my previously neglected food, cleaned off my table, and left to go back to the NICU. Walking back down the hall, I felt so much stronger than before. I held my head higher because I knew that God had placed him in my life. I knew that God was showing me that I was not alone, no matter how lonely it felt. I spent the entire remainder of the day by Bowen's bedside, watching, praying, and loving him as best I could.

Our days had begun to shift from sunny and bright to cloudy and gloomy right before our eyes. Overnight, his chest tube began to fail, allowing more air into his chest. It was replaced once again. Tube number four. His blood pressure, previously stable, began to drop drastically, causing him to restart a medication we had weaned him from once already. We desperately needed him to gain weight, but due to the continued surgeries, he had to pause feeds, receiving essential nutrients only through his umbilical line.

After numerous "how-are-you-doings" from family and friends, I shared my heart at the bottom of a Facebook status, following an update about Bowen. In it I wrote:

I am struggling, badly. I'm leaning hard on my faith, my family, and all of our friends. I cry a lot. I pray a lot. I worry a lot. Bowen is our rainbow baby, brought to us after a devastating loss and four years of infertility. It's only fitting that rainbows and storms go hand in hand, right? I am trying to find balance between being there for Bowen and being there for Sawyer and Dawson. A constant juggling act, and I just remembered I do not know how to juggle. The boys are sad. They're angry. They just want to love on their brother. We all do. We know God is in control. I feel guilty when I am overcome with worry and anxiety because I don't want it to seem as if I don't trust Him. I do. I know Bowen would not still be fighting without Him, and for that I am forever grateful. I search in my Bible for verses of encouragement regularly. We all just want Bowen to be healthy. To grow big and strong. To come home to join our family. We pray that he continues to fight for us, as we continue to go to the war room in prayer for him.

Bowen had been with us for one week. We celebrated by restarting feeds, reconfirming no new rain bleeds and no new chest tubes. Zach was juggling going to work, spending time at the NICU, and being present at home. But he was able to take the day off to celebrate with Bowen and me at the hospital. The tiniest accomplishments were the biggest victories, and we made sure to recognize and celebrate each one. *We are so in love with our tiny boy.* None of us were where we wanted to be, but we were exactly where we needed to be at the same time. We had a routine, a schedule. Bowen was making strides, and we cheered him on every step of the way. Sitting in two armchairs in the back of his room, we watched in awe as Bowen kicked his little feet around, earning the nickname "thumper." Nurses constantly came in to reposition him, creating small barriers in an attempt to stop him from sliding down his bed and messing with his ventilator. Stubborn like his mama, he attempted to pull out tubes and yank off wires while we watched. For such a tiny human, he was born with a fire roaring throughout him, and I knew right away he was going to change the world.

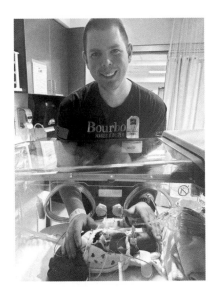

CHAPTER SEVENTEEN

The End of the Beginning

Friday, June 16, started off like any "normal" morning. I woke up, pumped breast milk for Bowen, packed my hospital bag, and got dressed. Right before we left, I went to the bathroom like I had every day prior, but today something was different. Standing at the sink washing my hands, I began to feel something on my stomach. It ran down into my pants before trickling down my leg. Flashbacks to my water breaking ran through my head as I frantically looked down. Blood. I gently lowered my shorts, softly lifted my shirt, and looked down at my stomach. Blood was everywhere. My eyes raised up to the mirror I was standing in front of, and like a scene from a scary movie, I saw blood pouring out of my C-section incision. It had reopened.

Panic immediately washed over me as I stood frozen in the bathroom, eyes glued to my reflection in the mirror. "Moooooommmmm!" I began to yell, "Help! I need help!" Quickly, she rushed into the bathroom, my sister Jessie still on FaceTime, and I was met with the same horrified reaction I was still experiencing.

"Sara's bleeding. I'll call you back." *Click.* We stood frozen in panic and disbelief as we began to plan our next moves. *I am eight days postpartum, this shouldn't be happening. What am I supposed to do with this!?* As my mom helped clean me up, I called my doctor's office for advice on what to do next. "Try to get the bleeding to stop. Place a pad on your incision site, and if you bleed through a pad in an hour, you need to go to the emergency room." Immediately, my panic began to shift. *Bowen. I need to go see Bowen. I can't go to the emergency room, I need to go to the NICU.* I needed the bleeding to stop so I could go see my baby. *I have a micro-preemie in the NICU, I can't be rehospitalized because of an open incision.* I did everything in my power to try and get the bleeding to stop, but after I bled through the initial pad in less than 20 minutes, I knew I needed to go to the ER. My sister Rachel was at my house for the weekend and agreed to watch Sawyer and Dawson so that Mom could take me to the emergency room.

This is not where I wanted to be today. We arrived at the hospital I had originally been admitted to and were taken back to a room right away. Staff wasted no time caring for me and the gaping hole in my stomach, temporarily closing the wound with butterfly bandages before thankfully agreeing to discharge me with strict instructions. Once again, I was told to rest, take it easy—whatever that means—and follow up immediately with my OBGYN. "Just another bump in the road," I told both my mom and myself, as we quickly went home before beginning our journey to the NICU. Our adventure that morning pushed back my NICU arrival time by about five hours, and we finally arrived shortly after lunchtime. I had missed hands-on time, something I looked forward to every day, but was thankful to be sitting in Bowen's hospital room instead of my own.

If you've ever sat in a hospital room, you know that it is stark and eerily quiet, while also being filled with the noises of machines, nurses coming in and out, bells, whistles, and beeps. Three separate times now, I had sat in an NICU room with one of my children. Each time, I was met with the same noises. The same chaos. The same quiet. When I close my eyes, I can still sometimes hear the beeping of the monitors. The sounding of the alarms when things start to go wrong. I can feel the calm chaos of the neonatal intensive care unit.

Per doctor's orders, I spent the majority of my day sitting in the chair by Bowen's bedside. The excitement of my incision reopening seemed to be the only big event of the day, and for that I was thankful. *I would take this all from him if I could.* Around five thirty in the evening, I pumped one final time, repacked my bag, and stood at his bedside, preparing to leave for the evening. Like every night, I began to pray over his tiny body. Immediately, I heard alarms. I opened my eyes, looked up at the screen where his vitals were, and watched as his numbers began to drop. Slow at first, then faster, dropping one after another. What was happening? He was *just* perfectly fine. His nurse was in the room with me. She had just finished writing down the numbers for his vitals, and I'd felt a sense of calm and comfort before leaving for the evening. In the blink of an eye, everything had changed. His pulse ox reading continued to drop at a concerning speed as I felt the familiar tingle of panic overcome me. I wanted nothing more than to rush to my child's aid, yet once again, I remained a helpless statue.

I stood by as doctors, nurses, and respiratory therapists ran into his room, a sight I was all too familiar with now. They shuffled around each other, almost like a dance, as they began to determine what had happened. In their attempt to stabilize him, I was once again pushed into a corner. Frozen. Internally I struggled, fighting back and forth with myself, trying to decide whether I should stay or go. On the outside, I was holding my breath, while on the inside I was screaming, unsure of what was happening around me. My mom and Rachel were waiting outside for me to go home with them, completely unaware of the terror I was experiencing just a few feet away.

The doctor quickly determined that he had yet another pneumothorax and would be requiring *another* chest tube. We assumed the tube he currently had needed to be replaced, maybe moved, and I exited to the waiting room once more. Between initial placements and replacement tubes, I had sat through this procedure five times already. I knew it took about an hour from start to finish, and I asked my mom and Rachel if they were okay waiting with me before we left. One hour came and went. Nothing. Rachel and I walked the halls. Two hours passed. Nothing. Mom, Rachel, and I did everything possible to distract ourselves. *What was taking so long?*

Hour three arrived before the double doors to the NICU opened again. The neonatologist tiredly walked out the doors, turned, and came towards me. My heart stopped as soon as I saw her. She was still wearing her surgical scrubs, her hair pulled back by a hairnet. Exhaustion radiated from her as she dropped down into the chair sitting empty between my mom and me. "You have some strong freaking kids," were the first words out of her mouth. Bowen had survived.

"I have never seen a baby his age or size survive what he just did, and he did awesome. His stats stayed stable the entire time. I had to call in a second doctor to help me. He ended up needing two new chest tubes on the right side. One on the top of his chest and one down lower." *Two chest tubes. A second neonatologist to help her.* The gravity of Bowen's condition really set in. I knew he was fragile and tiny. I knew he was sick, but up until then I had an unwavering confidence that no matter what, he would be fine. I withheld my tears as I walked back to his room, but sobbed over his bed as I saw him lying there, still alive.

A friend came to the hospital to pick up Rachel and take her home, while my mom and I were given a room in the NICU to stay the night. These rooms were reserved for special circumstances, and given how critical Bowen was, our family was allowed to stay. Zach sat impatiently at home, in a constant state of panic and worry, as my mom and I continued our night at the hospital. *I am here. I am just a few steps away. If anything happens, I am right here.* Struggling to get any rest, I chose instead to pray. My prayers continued nonstop throughout the night, praying that he would make it through the night and into the morning. I FaceTimed Zach and the boys as frequently as I could, sharing every tiny update we got.

Over the course of the night, Bowen seemed to be getting a little better. Zach and I started to hesitantly regain hope that he would turn a corner. Saturday was met with exhaustion from all sides. Zach and my mom swapped places early that morning, and together, we held hands as we sat tall and confident in Bowen's room. Our boy was doped up on so many medications to ease his pain and stabilize his blood pressure. A paralytic was administered to help him remain calm and still, aiding in his rest.

We now had to worry about his brain, given the extreme lack of oxygen he had continually experienced. *Brain damage and pneumothoraxes. Sawyer and Dawson. He is definitely a Schneider boy.* "He is the sickest and most critical baby we currently have," a nurse told us honestly when we asked about his condition. *Ouch, that stung.* Knowing something and hearing it confirmed to you out loud are two entirely different things.

Zach and I sat and watched Bowen all day Saturday. That afternoon, he began to improve, and by the evening, we felt confident enough to head home for the night. In the middle of the night, my phone rang. It was the neonatologist. "You need to come in," she said. "I think he blew another pneumothorax. This time on the left. I'm sitting in his room watching him now. His numbers are fluctuating, so we might be able to needle it out, but you and Zach should go ahead and come in. If we do the tube, it will be a last-ditch effort. I'll keep you updated. Drive safe." Zach and I jumped in the car and began our journey to Gainesville. To Bowen.

The doctor called again on the way: "I'm throwing a Hail Mary and putting him back on nitrous oxide. As of right now he doesn't seem to need a new tube, but we will see how this works." Entering the hospital, we had no idea what we would be walking into. The doctor met us right outside his room and motioned us inside. "Go look," she said. His pulse ox was reading 100. *Relief.* "Thank you, Jesus!" I began to cry. We sat with Bowen, marveling at his strength and God's mercy, before returning to the room the hospital gave my mom and me the night before. Another night closer to Bowen.

Weighed down with exhaustion, I was beginning to drift off when suddenly, I heard a knock on the door. The doctor walked in. "He needs the tube." The defeat on her face matched the feeling in my heart. "Go ahead and start to pray. I'll let you know when it's over." *Why was this happening again?* It was officially Father's Day, and something in my heart told me things were not going to be good. All day Sunday I held my breath, praying silently to myself that God would not take Bowen from us today, on Father's Day. A day meant to celebrate my husband as the amazing and loving father he is.

The left tube was placed successfully, but Bowen was extremely critical. Extremely sick. For the remainder of the night, Zach and I barely slept, dozing off only when we could no longer physically hold our eyes open. We had plans to have lunch with our families close by for Father's Day, but after the night we had, the idea of leaving now left us both in shambles. All morning, I prayed that we could celebrate Zach the way he deserved. Since his new chest tube was placed, Bowen seemed to be doing well, yet fear and anxiety began to seep into our minds and hearts.

During rounds late Sunday morning, Zach and I talked with the neonatologist who had arrived earlier that morning, after Bowen's surgery. In the corner of the NICU, surrounded by machines and computer screens, I began to confess my fears to her. Where once a confident, faithful mother had stood before her, I stood now as a fearful, anxious, scared mom, pleading with her to save my sons. My heart was weary. My soul was tired. My life had turned upside down.

Before Bowen was ever born, this doctor and I had had many conversations about my faith, and God's role in my children's lives. Looking at me, eyes filled with love and sincerity, she opened her mouth and said, "You've chosen to put your trust in God, so what do you have to fear?" She was right. Her words stuck to me like glue: a whisper from God, reminding me He was in control. Even still, her words, replaying through my mind, comfort me through moments of worry and fear, panic and anxiety. With a newfound hope and confidence, Zach and I mustered up the courage and energy to celebrate Father's Day with our family.

We picked a restaurant close to the hospital in an effort to sneak away for a few hours while remaining close by. Each moment we were gone, the weight on my chest got heavier and heavier. Each time a phone went off at lunch, every member of the family held their breath, regardless of what it was. We quickly finished our food, hugged the boys, and headed back to the hospital. On the way back, Zach and I talked about our game plan for the night. "Assuming Bowen remains stable, I'll go home tonight," Zach said, "I'll go to work early tomorrow morning and leave in time to pick you up from your doctor's appointment before going back to the NICU." I had my first incision follow-up appointment Monday, and we planned for a friend to drop me off.

The remainder of Father's Day was, thankfully, uneventful. Zach and I both felt confident with him going home, and right before dinner, we said our goodbyes. I stayed at the hospital again that night by myself, focusing all my energy and attention on Bowen. I gave Zach a kiss at the elevators before walking back to Bowen's room.

Sitting down in my chair in the corner, I watched in awe as Bowen lay still in the bed in front of me. The window behind me filled with dark, clear skies as moonlight poured into the room. A calm ambience hovered in the air. Overcome with love and emotions, I opened my mouth, and words began to pour out. I told him all about his family and the people who loved him. I told him about God. I shared the goodness of His grace, and how our faith had been carrying me. Tearfully, I told Bowen all about the people who continued to pray for him. I beamed with pride as I explained how proud I was of him, and the honor it was to be his mom. A nurse brought me books, and I sat and read to him, book after book, over and over, until I could barely keep my eyes open. In an attempt to freeze the moment, I picked up my phone, opened the camera, and began to videotape myself reading. I finally felt like I was able to mother him. I was spending quality time, experiencing a sleepless night with my baby for the first time since he was born. Shortly after midnight, I walked sleepily back to my room. A contented smile gently spread across my face, and a confidence I had been lacking flowed through me.

After the best night's sleep I had experienced in over a week, I woke up Monday morning ready to face the world. I would be leaving soon for my doctor's appointment, but first, I faced a conversation no parent ever wants to have: a conversation regarding our wishes should something go wrong again. Bowen currently had three chest tubes. He had blown more pneumothoraxes than anyone was prepared for, and we had faced one too many close calls. The cloud I had been floating on began to evaporate, and I came tumbling back down to reality. He seemed to have turned a corner towards healing, but still remained critical. We had to be prepared, *just in case.*

Despite the painful conversation I endured that morning, my confidence began to grow. Monday was easily one of the best days since Bowen's birth. He was calm. His numbers remained high and beautiful. He successfully received a PICC line, and for the first time, he opened his eyes and began to look around. I went to my first doctor's appointment since my incision reopened, where the inevitable was confirmed. Something that should be closed was open. Something that should be healed was not. I scheduled my follow-up appointment for the next morning and, per my doctor's request, promised to bring Zach so he could be taught how to pack the wound.

Monday brought so much joy. We had a game plan for my incision. Bowen was back on the right path. Zach and I had survived a weekend from hell, and saw the sun shining through the clouds of the previous few days. On Monday night, I went home for the first time since Friday. Keeping my phone on loud, I was prepared for another call to come through, rushing us right back out.

On Tuesday morning, I woke up feeling so peaceful. We did not receive a single call from the hospital overnight, and I had a confidence carrying me as I began to get ready for the day. I had another doctor's appointment for my incision, Zach had a retirement party at work for a mentor, and I just knew it was going to be a good day. Holding hands in the car, Zach and I sang along to the radio. We joked back and forth about his new job packing my wounds and talked about the day we were going to have. We were less than five minutes away from my doctor's office when my phone began to ring. A call that would change our lives forever. A number I did not have saved, yet looked eerily familiar. The hospital.

"Hey, Sara, its Mandy. Y'all need to come to the hospital. Bowen's not doing well. . . ." Something inside of me shifted, a seriousness I had never felt before taking over as I motioned down the road to Zach, signaling that we needed to go. Quick. He knew where. He knew why. He stepped on it, and we went. 12 days postpartum. Recovering from an emergency C-section. A gaping surgical wound four days reopened. None of that mattered. Zach circled around the front entrance of the hospital, dropping me off before parking. As soon as my feet hit the sidewalk, I ran. Full speed ahead; I needed to get to my son. The receptionist sitting at the NICU security desk saw me coming. She buzzed open the door before I even arrived. Turning the corner, I booked it inside. With no time to waste, I ran past the handwashing station, through the double doors, and down the hall. I turned the corner where his room was, and like a scene from a movie, everything seemed to be moving in slow motion. A flood of people hovering both inside and outside of his room.

This time was different. The wave of people parted as I arrived, making way for me inside. Nurses I had never seen before were trying and failing to pull air out of my tiny baby's body. The doctor turned around. Our eyes met, her face distraught, stricken with grief and pain. *She knew. I knew.* My body grew weak. Collapsing, I was caught by nurses and doctors before a familiar hand appeared on my back. Zach ran in right behind me. Uncontrollable sobs erupted from my body, and without speaking a word, Zach and I were able to communicate with each other that this was it. We knew we were not walking out of that room with our son alive ever again. Even with three chest tubes in his sides, his tiny lungs were too sick, too weak. He had blown another pneumothorax.

"You need to hold your son," the neonatologist told us. "We are running out of room to put tubes. He will keep blowing pneumos. We are torturing him. You need to hold your baby." *I can't do this. I can't do this.* **I cannot do this!** Zach, Karen, and our doctor helped lower me down into the chair in his room, the chair I'd spent countless hours in over the last 12 days. The chair I sang in. The chair I pumped in. The chair I read to my baby in. The chair I would soon hold him in. With the very last drop of strength remaining, Zach and I made the most impossible decision of our lives. We decided to hold Bowen. We knew another attempt at a chest tube would be unsuccessful torture.

We sat beside each other, tears streaming down our faces, listening to alarms beeping, a constant reminder of our reality. Chaos existed all around us as Bowen's team gently picked him up and brought him over to me. For the first time ever, my baby was in my arms where he belonged. Time stood still. The weight of his body in my arms filled my heart to the brim, while the finality of his life broke me to my core. Tears ran down my face, splashing on his tiny forehead. As I held him, I began to pray out loud. Stroking my finger against his leg, I prayed for his tiny, yet abundantly mighty, soul. Zach and I told him how proud we were of him. We told him how much we loved him. We told him how much God loved him. Not a dry eye existed in that space as we shared our love with our son.

At 8:59 a.m. on June 20, 2023, Bowen Walker Schneider took his final breath on earth before entering into the arms of Jesus. Zach and I watched in agony as medical equipment that just moments before had been keeping our son alive was packed up, tucked into his bed, and wheeled away. We mourned the loss of our tiny fighter, our hearts shattering into a million tiny pieces, never to be put back together again.

CHAPTER EIGHTEEN
Picking Up The Pieces

Nobody tells you about the decisions that come immediately after the loss of a loved one. Extreme grief is met with the unfair assumption of your ability to make immediate, permanent decisions. How and when will you tell people? Will you have a funeral? Will you bury them, and if so, where? What about cremation? Questions no parent ever dreams of having to answer soon needed almost immediate responses. Bowen had just been declared dead by the doctor, and Zach and I watched as the staff began to wheel his bed out of his room. Our life had broken into two distinct parts: Part one, a family of five. Happy, healthy, alive. Three boys we would watch grow. Our future. Part two, a broken family. Two children alive on earth, one healed in the arms of Jesus. A family that would never be the same again. Dreams of the future died along with Bowen. Who he would be, what hobbies he'd have, graduations, weddings—all of it, gone. The people we were before Bowen died were gone forever, and standing before us were strangers. Heartbroken strangers, drenched in tears, left to pave the way for the future of our family.

Zach, being the amazing caregiver he is, immediately jumped into action. He began calling our families to deliver the horrible news, and making arrangements for our parents and the boys to come to the hospital to meet Bowen. We began to mentally prepare ourselves to tell Sawyer and Dawson about the death of their baby brother, shuddering at the thought of breaking their little hearts just as ours had been just moments prior. I was holding Bowen skin to skin, and the bereavement team asked if we wanted to follow them to a private room to be with our now unalive son. My legs were weak with grief as I stood up, clutching gently onto the son I had just said goodbye to. The weight of Bowen's lifeless body filled my arms as we began down the hall to a private room where we would spend the rest of the day together. We rounded the hall, eyes blurry with tears, and walked inside. Two recliners, a table in the corner, and two chairs sat empty as we entered. This was it, the place where we would begin the second part of our lives, the part without Bowen. The room in which we would break the news to our boys about their brother. The room where we would decide how to bury our child. The room where we would tell our friends and family of his passing. The room where we would see our son this side of Heaven for the very last time.

Soon, people began to show up. First, Zach's parents. I sat in the chair as my mother and father-in-law entered our room. Slowly, they walked over to us, crying, hugging, and repeating how sorry they were for our loss. Not long after their arrival, the bereavement team came to clean Bowen up. Still dangling from his perfect skin were the remains of the chest tubes. Carefully, I handed my boy over, and a few moments later, he returned, ready to be bathed. I steadied myself before walking over to the isolette to bathe him for the first and last time. Gently, I dipped the washcloth into the bath and brought it to his arm. Picking up his arm, for the first time I was able to truly see the lifelessness of his body as he lay still before me. No twitching, no moving. Where he would previously wrap his tiny fingers around mine, lay a perfectly still hand. I broke.

Overcome with grief, my knees buckled beneath me as tears began to pour down my face. My weight resting on the isolette holding Bowen, I began to wail. He was gone, he was really gone. No twitching like I saw after Sawyer's resuscitation, no movement in his once-active hands and feet. Instead, I was met with the harsh reality of his death in a way I had not yet anticipated. Bowen was dead, and he would not be coming back.

A few hours later, my mom and the boys arrived from Alabama. With childlike wonder and excitement, Sawyer and Dawson rushed into the room. "Bowen!" They yelled, upon entering, no question as to why they were there. They had no idea of the events that had taken place that morning, and instead were eager to finally meet their baby brother in person. As they entered the room, Sawyer caught a glimpse of my face, halting in his tracks. My mom walked over to the side of the room and, for the first time all day, had the freedom to break down. She had been strong for the boys as they drove from Alabama back to the hospital four hours away, and finally let it all out.

Sliding down the wall, she fell into a puddle on the floor, head in hands, shoulders shaking, and tears flowing as she began to mourn the loss of her grandson. I redirected my attention to the boys, a knot the size of a mountain forming in my throat. The moment I had been dreading all day had arrived as I began to choke out the words, "Bowen died this morning," to the boys. The second the words left my lips, I wished I could take them back. *Why was this happening?!* As a mom, I wanted nothing more than to protect my children, and in that moment, I felt like I had failed each one of them.

Dawson, filled with innocence and confusion, did not quite understand. He was two weeks from his fifth birthday, and the idea of death was nothing he had personally experienced before. "Will he be alive again in three days like Jesus?" he asked. Heartbreakingly, we told him no, and "Oh, will it be four days then?" left his lips. Sawyer, wise beyond his years, immediately burst into tears, crying heavier than I had ever experienced before. My heart broke all over again. He understood. I did this. I broke his heart. Immense guilt filled my soul as I cried with him. "I'm so sorry,"

I repeated over and over as I held him close, wishing I could take the pain away from him.

We spent the remainder of the day loving on Bowen, taking pictures as a family, and spending our last day on earth with him. My dad arrived at the hospital, and for the first and last time ever, we were able to create family pictures together. Each of us took time to hold Bowen, give him kisses, and memorize his features. A gentle smile seemed to rest across his face, and I knew he was safe in the arms of Jesus.

Quicker than any of us could ever be ready, it was time to say our goodbyes. One by one, Zach and I said goodbye to the boys and our parents, sending them on their way before spending our final moments alone with Bowen. Bowen in my arms, and me in Zach's, we huddled over one another for the last time. A knock on the door came sooner than we wanted, and we knew it was time. Zach and I had chosen to have Bowen cremated so that we could bring him home to us, and a funeral home was chosen and called. The chaplain walked into our room to let us know the funeral home director had arrived to take Bowen with him, and after a final goodbye, we sobbed as we handed our son over to them. His tiny body was placed in a beautiful woven basket before being carried off, alone, one last time. Zach and I erupted into sobs, leaning on one another, as the sight of our son vanished from our eyes forever. For the final time, we began our exit from the hospital. No baby. No smiles. Instead, empty, bloodstained blankets and irreparable hearts were all that we took with us.

The days following Bowen's death were an emotional blur, creating memories both vague and sharp at the same time. Our home quickly filled with family who came from all across the country to be by our side. Food was delivered, and on more than one occasion, I was being fed by someone who loved me, as I was too weak to feed myself. With my incision still open, I was shuffled to and from the doctor's in an attempt to heal my physical wound, while my emotional scars were ripped so far open I felt as if they would never heal, nor did I want them to. The idea of healing, at the time, felt like moving on. How could I heal? How could I ever move on? I did not want to heal. I did not want to move on. I wanted my baby. I longed to sit in the NICU, attempting to get comfortable in the stiff chair, watching as monitors beeped, signaling life in Bowen's body.

Instead, I visited the funeral home to pick out tiny urns, and began making arrangements for a funeral I never wanted to attend. The first time we went to the funeral home was the day after Bowen passed. In order to perform the cremation, we had forms to sign and decisions to be made. Zach and I knew we could not do this alone, and together, we decided to ask one of the strongest people we knew to go along with us: my dad. Zach and my dad helped me into the car, and we started down the road. Clutching Bowen's knit blue baby blanket, I attempted to mentally prepare myself for what was about to happen. We had driven past this funeral home many times before, even attending community events on its lawn on more than one occasion. This time, however, was different. We turned in not to ride carnival rides or buy deep fried goodies, but instead to make arrangements for our son. Parking, we began our journey to the front doors. As we reached the entrance, a wave of emotion knocked me over, and I fell into the arms of my dad and my husband. My legs quit working, not allowing me to go any further. Gently and lovingly, the two most amazing men in my life began to lead me inside and down the hall to a room filled with urns and casket catalogs. Dad held my hand and asked questions, Zach signed paperwork, and I sat frozen, attempting to breathe through tears, pain, and heartache.

On June 25, 2023, we laid our son to rest. Dressed in black, we arrived at our church, unprepared for the events about to transpire. Entering the building, we were welcomed by a sea of family, friends, and hospital staff who had traveled from near and far to pay their respects. Blind with grief, we walked inside, finding our seats at the front of the sanctuary. A beautiful table sat in front of us. Flowers, pictures, and Bowen's beads of courage draped across on display, and at the center: Bowen's urn. The tiniest urn I had ever laid eyes on, its contents holding open the gaping hole in my heart. The service was a beautiful declaration of God's love, even through grief and heartache. A eulogy was bravely delivered by my sister Jessie, accompanied by Dawson, before videos and beautifully written messages of love and condolence from our family and friends began to play on the screens in the sanctuary.

Videos of people in attendance, accompanied by those who could not make the service, played before us as we sat in awe of the love being showered over our family. A photographer stood nearby, lovingly taking pictures of the service, creating lifelong memories of a day we never wanted to experience, yet never wanted to forget. The service ended, and Zach and I bravely rose to our feet to face the love and support we were receiving head-on. Soon, we were met with a crowd larger than we could have ever imagined. A line wrapping around the entire sanctuary began to form as co-workers, nurses, doctors, friends, family, and strangers came up to us. The impact our son had made in his 12 short days of life brought a sense of pride unexplainable, especially in a time of grief, and for the first time, we knew his story was not over. Bowen, whether on earth or in Heaven, was created for a reason, and it was up to us to share his life and story with the world.

Part Four

CHAPTER NINETEEN

In Sickness and In Health

My sophomore year of college, I was sitting on my best friend's couch eating pizza when I got a text from one of my sorority sisters. She told me her boyfriend's roommate had just adopted a puppy, and that I had to come meet him. Before I could decide whether or not I was going, a second text came through. "Also, his roommate thinks you're cute." For some reason, the thought of a boy thinking I was cute made me question whether or not I actually wanted to go. The idea of dating honestly seemed like too much work at the time, and I was content living my best single-girl life.

I went back and forth on the idea for a few minutes before deciding I would drive over there, meet the puppy, and go on with my day. "You're making this a much bigger deal than necessary," I convinced myself. "So what if he thinks you're cute? Go meet the puppy and go home." I finished my pizza, got in my car, and drove to the apartment to meet my friend. I had let go of all thoughts of the mystery boy who thought I was cute and was focused on one thing: puppies.

I parked my car, texted my friend that I was there, walked down the stairs to the main floor apartment, and rounded the corner to the front door. As soon as I arrived, the door swung open. Standing in the doorframe was a tall guy with blue-green eyes. Dark brown hair fell out from underneath a backwards baseball hat. He was wearing jeans and cowboy boots, and my heart skipped a beat. In his arms was a tiny puppy, brown and white, with the sweetest face I had ever seen. I knew then that I was in trouble. "Hi, I'm Zach," he started, "and this is Kross." He motioned to the puppy. I was done. We spent the rest of the night talking, laughing, and getting to know each other.

That night, it snowed. In Georgia, we don't get much snow, but this night we did. In fact, we got so much snow that the city of Atlanta shut down. People were abandoning their cars on the interstate, schools were cancelled, and stores had closed. For the next week, Zach, his roommate, my friend, myself, Kross, and the roommate's dog were trapped in their tiny basement apartment. By the time the ice and snow began to melt, I knew my heart belonged to someone else. I arrived at that apartment uninterested in dating. A week later, I left knowing I had found my person, and we have been together ever since.

From the day I met Zach, we talked about what a future together would look like. This included the potential of a future family. That first conversation, Zach and I both discussed the dream we had of having three children. We talked about our families, finding out that we both only had sisters, and mentioned that we both knew we wanted to be boy parents one day. We shared our goals, hopes, and dreams. We talked about what we wanted to be as we got older, where we wanted to travel, and the lives we wanted to live. Over the next ten months of our relationship, we fell more in love each day than the day before. We both knew we wanted to spend the rest of our lives together, and on December 13, 2014, Zach asked me to marry him.

Waking up that morning, I had no idea where the day would take me. My sister Jessie was in town for the weekend, and when I woke up, I found a note by my bed. Zach was nowhere to be found, my phone was gone, and the note explained that I was going on a scavenger hunt. Each clue I found had instructions leading me to my next destination. At each stop, I found one of my friends with my next clue, leading me one step closer to forever. Over the course of the day I had breakfast, got both my hair and makeup done, bought a new outfit, had lunch, and shared the excitement and anticipation of what was to come with the people I loved most. Finally, I arrived at the lake close to where we met. Standing down by the water was Zach. Anxiously, I made my way down to him. My heart beat fast, tears flowing from my eyes, and the hope of the future carried me through each step. Once I arrived, Zach grabbed me by the hands, professed his love for me, got down on one knee, and asked me to marry him. To be completely honest, I was crying so hard, I did not hear a word of what he said. The excitement and love I felt overwhelmed me so much that the next thing I knew, he was asking, "Is that a yes?" *"Yes!"* I yelled back through tears of joy!

The following October, surrounded by our family and friends, I walked down the aisle to my best friend. We had planned a perfect, outdoor fall wedding in the North Georgia mountains. For a week leading up to our wedding, it rained. Mud puddles, flood warnings, and the threat of severe storms did their best to ruin our day, but as we have learned throughout the course of our relationship, no storm alone has the power to tear us apart. Quickly, we moved the ceremony inside our reception area. A few hours later, we said "I do."

We wasted no time starting our family. Just six months after we got married, I found out I was pregnant with Sawyer. At just 21 years old, I did not know what I was doing, but what I did know was that I wanted to be a mother more than absolutely anything. Over the course of the next nine months, we excitedly began to prepare ourselves for this next chapter of our lives. As we have come to find out time and time again, however, the plans we make for ourselves and God's plans are not always on the same wavelength. Sometimes, it feels as if we aren't even in the same ocean. Something Zach and I have decided along the way is that we chose each other. We chose each other as two strangers standing face to face in the dimly lit apartment hallway. We chose each other on the lakeshore in December. We chose each other that rainy day in October, and we would choose each other each and every day following.

We were not prepared for the complications that building our family would involve. We never imagined the outcome of Sawyer's birth. Or Dawson's. Or Bowen's. We never dreamt of having to juggle neurology appointments, eye surgeries, countless therapists, and three NICU stays. Never in our wildest dreams did we ever fathom planning a funeral for one of our children. What we did do, however, was decide that we would do it all together. When Sawyer was born, we stood hand in hand and took on the world. When Dawson was born, we held each other up as we tackled the NICU again. When we found out about my ectopic pregnancy, we confided in one another about our fears and worries. When Bowen was born, we pulled ourselves up by our bootstraps and did it all again, and when Bowen passed, we knew more than ever before that we needed each other.

I'm not saying it has always been easy; it hasn't. Each NICU stay brought new challenges. Each challenge brought new disagreements, and each disagreement brought new heartache. There were times I was not sure we would make it, but each time we encountered a new obstacle, we asked ourselves one question: Do we want this? Each time, the answer was yes. We knew we wanted to be together. We knew we loved each other, and we knew that no matter what life threw at us, we could stand tall, hand in hand, knowing we had each other. In sickness and in health. In good times and in bad. Till death do us part.

CHAPTER TWENTY
It Takes a Village

As a parent, you are told time and time again that "it takes a village." What does this even mean? Finding "your people" seems impossible. Community is what God calls us to, but oftentimes it feels like a daunting task. We are left searching for a sense of community while struggling to keep our heads above water, exhausted from the day-to-day demands of life. Add in the daily struggles of motherhood and being a good spouse, all while trying to juggle the never-ending cycle of laundry piling up in the other room, and we are left exhausted, overstimulated, and desperate for a sliver of quiet. The very idea of creating a sense of community at times seems like more work than it's worth. Yet no matter the work that might go into it, we pray for that very sense of belonging. That coveted idea of community. We long to belong, and to be loved. We want nothing more than for our kids to be accepted, dreaming of the types of relationships you can raise your family with. We want the community to which we are called to create and nurture.

I got lucky with my community. The shutdown of 2020 taught my family, like many others, one very important truth: We had outgrown our home. We were fortunate enough to be able to act on this newfound information, and in November of 2020 we packed up and moved 15 minutes down the road. While we remained geographically close, this move opened up a whole new world for our family. We joined a new church, created new friends, and immersed ourselves in a community that welcomed us with open arms. Our friends quickly turned into family, and in the moments I needed them most, they showed up for me in ways I never anticipated. Our pain is their pain. Our struggles became their struggles. Our loss became their loss.

Immediately after I was hospitalized with Bowen, my village showed up. While we were still in the doctor's office, a friend swooped in and took the boys for us. Immediately after we received the news of my incompetent cervix, both Zach's phone and mine began to blow up. Dozens of messages and phone calls poured in: offers of prayer, words of encouragement, and petitions to help in any way possible. Without hesitation, the children's pastor at our church headed to the hospital to pick up Sawyer and Dawson, dropping them off at a second friend's house as they waited for my mom to arrive and take over. We had people take time to come to sit at the hospital with me so I would not be alone, and from the first moment a need arose, we didn't have to ask for help with Sawyer and Dawson. Friends, family, and neighbors alike joined in to take care of our dogs just so Zach could be at the hospital with me as much as possible. Friends and acquaintances I had not spoken to for over a decade reached out. Our village took care of us. They prayed, gathered, and fed us. Each and every one of them exhibited the love of Christ, cultivating breathtakingly beautiful examples of what He calls us to do within our community.

When I could not physically hold myself up after Bowen's passing, there were people to hold me up. When I could do nothing but cry, there were people to cry right alongside me. I couldn't bear the thought of being alone, and I didn't have to be because my people showed up. As I sit and look back on those first moments, I can't help but be overcome with gratitude for the people whom God placed in my life. Just as I had been clinging to the truths of Romans 12:12, I was graciously greeted with the scriptures surrounding it. "Love must be sincere. Hate what is evil; cling to what is good. Be devoted to one another in love. Honor one another above yourselves. Never be lacking in zeal, but keep your spiritual fervor, serving the Lord. Be joyful in hope, patient in affliction, faithful in prayer. Share with the Lord's people who are in need. Practice hospitality" (Romans 12:9–13).

One month to the day after Bowens's passing, we found ourselves back in the hospital. Zach had to have emergency gallbladder removal surgery. The pain I felt watching my husband mixed with the emotion of emergency surgery and extreme grief quickly became overwhelming; however, I was not alone. The hospital chaplain, Karen, who was in the operating room the day Bowen was born—the same one who held us tight the day he passed—came to the hospital and sat by my side during his surgery. She prayed with us, she talked with us, and she sat with us.

After hearing about Zach's hospitalization, one of Bowen's nurses from the NICU came up to the hospital on her day off so that I would not be alone while my husband was in surgery. She prayed with me. She laughed and talked with me. She distracted me and was there for me in a way that was so Christ-centered that I will never forget it, and always cherish it. Friends from church kept the boys from sunup to sundown so that I could stay at the hospital with Zach. Both my parents and Zach's helped us around the clock, ensuring that we both had everything we needed. For the third time in a month, we could not do it alone, and our people showed up.

Life after loss is hard. While certain moments seem so clear that I can close my eyes and be right back in them, there were other moments where Zach and I both were just . . . existing. Fragments of our lives exist where I don't exactly know how we got through the next minute, much less the whole day. The love and support of our community carried us through. God placed exactly the right people in our lives at exactly the right moments so that we could continue on. People we had never met before fed us, preparing food for us as well as stocking our fridge and pantry. We had neighbors show up to cut our grass and do our laundry. I never fully understood the phrase "it takes a village" until a village was sent to me in a time when I needed it most. Thanks to the amazing village we've been blessed with, we were able to focus on our grief. On our pain. On our boys. On ourselves. I can confidently say that the people who helped guide us through the deepest trenches of our grief were sent directly from God, and I know He sent us some of the very best people He has.

CHAPTER TWENTY-ONE

Golfing With Giraffes

The night Sawyer was born, I knew he was born for a reason. The day Dawson was born, I knew he was born for something special. The day Bowen was born, I knew he would change the world. I might not have wanted or ever dreamt of this life, but I knew immediately that I was chosen as their mom for something greater. The first time we experienced the power of their lives was when Dawson was only eight months old. A representative from the hospital's medical foundation had heard about our story and reached out to me, hoping to interview our family for their newsletter. We talked to the reporter, took family pictures, and were able to share the miracle of our two boys. Over the course of the next three years, we worked closely with the foundation. I was invited to sit in on and speak at board meetings. The foundation gave me the opportunity to talk about the importance of the care Sawyer and Dawson had received and the impact the NICU had on the structure of our family, as well as a platform to share my story.

On May 17, 2022, Zach, Sawyer, Dawson, and I attended the Laurel Classic Golf Tournament at *Chateau Elan*. We had been anticipating and helping plan this event for almost three years, and the day had finally arrived. The moment we arrived at the golf course, we were treated like royalty. Sawyer and Dawson were awarded the opportunity to kick off the tournament with the ceremonial tee-off as our family was recognized by hospital board members. Following the conclusion of the tournament, we attended the closing ceremonies and silent auction. With shaking knees and a flip-flopping stomach, I bravely made my way up to the front of the room, grabbed the microphone, and peered out at all the people eagerly looking my direction. Taking a deep breath, I stood up tall, gathered my confidence, and began to speak. I told the room about Sawyer's birth. I explained the low chance of survival he was given, and the level of care we received both during and after his birth. I talked about Dawson's birth, and being back in the same NICU, in the same room I watched my son leave just 19 months prior.

A lump formed in my throat as I began to glorify God and the miracles He had performed in their lives. I acknowledged the abilities of the hospital staff and thanked the board for the community that had been established by the hospital system. The lifesaving technology and materials the NICU had obtained were a significant part of why my boys were both here today, and I made sure the importance of them was acknowledged. My speech ended; I exhaled deeply, wiped the tears forming in my eyes away, and made my way back to my seat as applause erupted all around me.

Over $275,000 was raised during that event, an impact I never anticipated would circle back to me or my family. Part of the money raised went to purchase new giraffe beds for the NICU. These specialized beds create a structured, controlled, and stress-free environment for babies. Babies in this space experience life similar to that in their mother's womb. Each bed costs about $36,000, and knowing we were part of raising money for these beds brought a sense of joy and accomplishment to our family. It was not until Bowen was born that we truly understood or felt the importance of the tournament.

A few days after Bowen was born, Zach and I found ourselves standing in Bowen's hospital room. His nurse began explaining to us all what the bed he was in did. She went into detail about the environment they were able to create for these babies and the simulation of the mother's womb they would experience. A lightbulb went off in our heads. We looked to the top of the bed, and there we saw it. Sitting on top of the lid and looking right back at us was the giraffe, the same giraffe we helped raise money for just two years prior. A true full-circle moment—Zach and I were able to feel for the first time that we were doing something to help take care of Bowen.

We'd started sharing the story in 2018. We'd planned, rescheduled, and replanned the tournament through a global pandemic. The courage

I'd mustered as I stood in front of a room full of strangers and shared our story all came back to this moment. This is what it is all about: the babies. When we agreed to help all those years ago, we never could have anticipated we would also be on the receiving end of this support. Every time we walked into Bowen's room, we saw the giraffe and smiled. His family was forever with him, even when we could not physically be there. His brothers helped take care of him indirectly through their support. The love of our community enveloped him at all times.

CHAPTER TWENTY-TWO
Faith Through Failure

The day Bowen passed, I knew that our family would need help. The pain of his loss enveloped us completely. Dark clouds came barreling in, our previously sunny demeanor masked entirely by his loss. I knew that we would not be able to navigate this newfound grief alone. As questions and decisions quickly arose, Zach jumped right in, handling the state of our finances, insurance claims, and all the logistics. I turned another way. Divide and conquer, something we had become professionals at throughout our parenthood journey.

Knowing my husband would handle the concrete, I shifted my focus to the mental and emotional, immediately setting out to find the help and resources I knew we would all need. Unfortunately, it seemed almost too easy to find things we might need for Zach and myself when it came to the grief of losing our child. Almost instantly, we were pointed in the right directions. Support groups, therapists, like-minded individuals, books—you name it, we *thankfully* could find it. Before we even left the hospital the day Bowen died, I had a list overflowing with helpful, positive resources for us.

When it came to Sawyer and Dawson's grief, however, it was a completely different story. Finding a children's grief therapist who had any experience with the loss of a sibling was next to impossible. Support groups for kids who had experienced this trauma and loss were nonexistent. I struggled daily with how to parent *through* grief. I struggled with how to parent *to* grief. Not only was I lost in grief myself, drowning with the pain of losing my son, but I was also helping guide two small children, blindly leading them through something I did not fully understand as an adult.

Sleepless nights were something I had become accustomed to. The funeral was over, family and friends had all gone home, and the quiet of the nights became too much to bear. When thoughts of Bowen weren't running through my mind, Sawyer and Dawson were. In a moment of extreme weakness, I began to break down. Hyperventilating, sobbing and spiraling, I found myself calling my dad. In the middle of the night, my phone rang. Tears streamed down my face as I tried to steady my breath. The ringing stopped, and I was instantly comforted by the sound of my dad's voice on the other end of the line. "Dad, I don't know what to do," I began. Tears flowing faster, my breath becoming more frantic, I began to panic again. "I feel like I'm failing them. I don't know what boundaries to set. I don't know where I should be lenient and where I should be firm. Parenting is hard enough, I don't know what to do."

Through my panic, he calmly confirmed that what I was feeling was right—to an extent. Parent *is* hard enough without obstacles. When you throw a major obstacle like grief into an already delicate balance, it seems impossible. My grief mixed with the grief of my children made me feel like I was sinking and there was no way out. The frustration I was encountering kept circling back to one thing: I felt alone. Not in my marriage, or with my family or friends—my personal support system was great—but as a bereaved mother navigating parenting after loss. I felt as if my kids were being cheated and nobody cared to help them. My dad and I talked on the phone that night for over an hour. He reassured me, helped me breathe again, and positively affirmed that I was doing the best I could. This grief was new to all of us, and together, we would survive.

Bowen's passing occurred over summer break, but soon we found ourselves preparing for and attending back-to-school events for the boys. Dawson, now in kindergarten, was set to attend the same school he was at the year prior. The staff at the small, private Christian school already knew about Bowen's birth, life, and death. Walking through the parking lot toward his open house, I knew our loss had been talked about and prayed over, and that we would be supported. Taking a deep breath, I pulled open the door and was greeted by smiling teachers and the school director. Lovingly, the staff pulled me into a tight hug, and I immediately knew that no matter what Dawson might need, he was in the right place. His teachers were aware of our loss, and not having to explain the situation we were in made everything so much easier. One down, one to go.

Sawyer was starting out at a brand-new school, and I needed a game plan. The day of his open house, I walked in confident and with a purpose. I knew I needed to inform his teacher of the tragedy that our family had experienced over the summer. Hand in hand, we found his classroom, walked in together, and introduced ourselves with smiles on our faces. I finished filling out all of the forms, and as Zach and Sawyer left to explore his new school, I pulled his teacher to the side. *I can do this*, I thought to myself. With as much confidence as possible, I began to give her a brief synopsis of our loss. Without an ounce of hesitation, I was met with immeasurable amounts of grace and love from someone I had just met. Not only did we set in place a game plan for Sawyer should a need arise, but she also made a conscious effort to check on how I personally was doing. I walked out of her classroom feeling so much love, gratitude, and confidence.

The next stop on my list was the school counselor. After only a few wrong turns and unexpected detours, I found who I was looking for. Once again, I took a deep breath, introduced myself, and began to recite the speech I had just performed to Sawyer's teacher, a speech I had repeated to myself hundreds of times in preparation for this event. I began explaining how we had lost Bowen just a few weeks prior, and before I knew it, she was pulling me in for a hug. The biggest sigh of relief exited my body as I was once again feeling a level of love, acceptance, and comfort I could never have anticipated from complete strangers.

Not long after the school year began, we had our first run-in with the lack of education and resources that comes along with sibling loss. A school project: creating a family portrait. Sawyer boldly asked, in front of a class full of first graders, if he could "draw his dead brother." Unfortunately, and through no fault of her own, the teacher whom he asked this to was *not* aware of our loss. Understandably, she was truly left speechless and did not know the appropriate way to handle the situation. My husband and I were quickly made aware of what had happened and soon met with the teacher, as well as the principal, and were able to share our story and Bowen's life. The loving, accepting, compassionate staff at his school cried with us as we shared that yes, Sawyer does in fact have a "dead brother." Immediately, they recognized that there wasn't a plan in place for these types of losses, and I was invited to come speak to the faculty.

Accepting the request and ability to share our story, as well as provide research and education to the entire faculty, was a no-brainer for me, and without an ounce of hesitation, I agreed. We all agreed we would be naive to think that my boys would be the last to lose a sibling. It was obvious that a need was not being met. That interaction allowed us to take a step towards changing the narrative, stigma, and lack of education surrounding child and sibling loss. I immediately rushed home and began to prepare. A few weeks later, I returned to his school and spoke at a faculty meeting. I talked about Bowen. I talked about Sawyer and Dawson and the grief they had been experiencing. I spoke about the lack of support siblings receive after the loss of a brother or sister, and in that moment, I knew God was speaking to me. He was calling me, through my grief, to make a change.

CHAPTER TWENTY-THREE

Calling Over Comfort

H ave you ever felt God calling you to do something over and over and over again? Yet instead of dropping everything and following Him, you continue to look for signs that it's *really* what He wants you to do? I know I have. In all honesty, when this happens, you *know* that the pull is directly coming from God, but it's not what you would have expected Him to call you to do. It's not what you would have chosen for yourself, and it's *absolutely* out of your comfort zone.

If I'm being honest with myself, this exact battle has been my life the last seven and a half years. Growing up, I always claimed that it took a "special type of person" to care for and be the parent of a special-needs child. While I held, and still hold, the utmost respect for these families, I did not think it could ever be me. Thinking back on it, I always claimed that I was "not capable" of doing *most* of the things that God has brought me to do. Almost immediately after Sawyer was born, the desire to write a book about his birth and God's hand in it was placed on my heart. I searched high and low for every possible excuse not to do it, partially out of laziness, but mostly out of fear. I'm no writer, I continued to tell not only myself but Him as well. I searched for any possible way to position my comfort level over the calling He had placed on my heart. I went so far as to attempt to bargain with God about this. When I was first admitted to the hospital with incompetent cervix during my pregnancy with Bowen, I told Zach that *if* Bowen and I both survived this, *then* I would write the book. Ouch. Admitting it even now is so embarrassing, but that's who we are as humans, right? I know that's not how God works, and I knew the conditions I had been proposing were far from fair. I was attempting to bargain with God, crying out to Him and saying that *if* He saved my life and *if* He saved my son's life, *then* I would follow Him and His plans.

Who am I to bargain with God? Who am I to try to convince Him one way or another? Who am I to try and come up with a compromise worthy of His mercy? Laying in that hospital room, I reasoned with Him that I would listen if He first gave me something that I wanted. As a parent, I know firsthand how frustrating that is. Sawyer and Dawson try to reason with me, doing the exact same thing I tried with God, all while I am left wondering why they can't just follow the simple directions that I gave them. How convicting is that?

As a child growing up in church, I learned about Jonah. Any kid who has grown up attending Sunday school can tell you all about Jonah and the big fish. I always thought of Jonah as a funny story, thinking about what life inside the belly of a fish would be like rather than the lesson it was teaching us. It wasn't until I became an adult that I revisited and began studying his story, and truly started to relate to his attempt to run from God.

Jonah had a calling. He had a direct order from God, and instead of following what he had been called to do, he chose, or attempted to choose, the easy way out. He attempted to run from God. He attempted to hide and disregard what God had called him to do. *How silly was he to try to run and hide from God?* I used to ask myself. It wasn't until I was sitting in my hospital bed and those words came out of my mouth that it smacked me right in the face. *I was Jonah.* I had known for years now what God had called me to do. I witnessed a real-life miracle in my son, and here I was, trying to hide and bargain rather than bring glory to the

One responsible. Almost as soon as the words left my mouth, a whisper began to echo through my head. I would write the book *either way*. I would bring God glory *either way*. *His calling outweighs my comfort.*

I'm not sure about you, but I can confidently say I am a flawed, sin-filled human. I am so incredibly accustomed to things within my realm of comfort that oftentimes I find myself going out of my way to avoid disturbing it. Without even realizing, I caught myself striving to do things within my comfort zone, so much so that I almost missed out on the entire purpose of my life.

Choosing what God has called me to do has not been easy. In fact, more often than not, I feel like I have absolutely no idea what I am doing. What I have learned along the way is that that's totally okay, and I am not alone. In my role as a wife, I am relying on grace not only from my husband, but from God as well. In motherhood, I am almost always winging it. As the founder of a nonprofit organization, I pray before every single task is done because I rarely feel as if I *actually* know what I'm doing. As an author, I do my best to articulate myself while secretly hoping that the words I write down make sense.

God called me to be Zach's wife. God called me to be Sawyer, Dawson, and Bowen's mother. God called me to start the Bowen Walker Foundation. God called me to write this book. I live outside of my comfort zone each and every single day that I follow His will and plan for my life, yet in those moments of fear and discomfort, I feel the most safe. I am wrapped in the arms of the Lord in the moments where I truly have no idea what I am doing. Sometimes, we are called to take a leap of faith, and I chose to jump. Taking a deep breath, I turned to God, filled with more confidence than ever before, and jumped, confident that He would catch me.

CHAPTER TWENTY-FOUR

Bowen Walker Foundation

I left the school faculty meeting and began walking to my car, my heart filled with a new hope. A new purpose. Sitting in the parking lot of Sawyer's school, I called Zach. Before I knew it, I found myself telling him that God was calling me to something bigger, and that I needed to start a nonprofit for children who had lost siblings. I had no idea what I was doing, or of the amount of work that would go into this, or even if it would succeed, but none of that mattered. I knew God had called me to it, and I blindly and boldly chose to follow Him. Not long after that meeting, the Bowen Walker Foundation was born.

The goal of the Bowen Walker Foundation is to serve bereaved parents and siblings who are experiencing child loss. Since our founding, we have had the opportunity to serve bereaved families through pregnancy loss, stillbirth, infant loss, and adolescent child loss. As an organization, we strive to provide personal and community-wide education, support, and resources to both the families we serve and the communities we live in. We know we cannot make the loss of these children any easier, so instead we strive to create a more attainable plan of action. We want to give back to others in the ways we longed for after our loss.

Starting a nonprofit was never in my plan. I have always loved volunteering. Growing up, I never shied away from an opportunity to give back to my community and would lend a helping hand in any way that I could, but I never expected this type of work to be something I was called to do, something so incredibly close to my heart. I want to be able to provide schools with the education and resources they need so that they can form and curate appropriate responses to future children grieving a great loss. I want to be able to create a sense of belonging and community, not only for parents who have experienced the loss and death of a child, but also for the children living with only tales and memories of their siblings, siblings who should be growing up right alongside them. I want to change the narrative surrounding child loss.

So many children around us are struggling with grief. Each child's grief not only varies from person to person, but it also varies within them drastically. Grief in children grows with them, and it's something that they hold their entire lives. As Sawyer and Dawson have grown in their grief, we have experienced this change firsthand. Things that never crossed Sawyer's mind early on in grief, he now experiences in a new way. Memories of Bowen that Dawson used to smile at now make him cry. Grief is not something we get through, but instead something that becomes part of us. It shifts, changes, and evolves as time goes on. Grief is surprising, jumping out at you when you least expect it, and to think our children do not experience these intense feelings and emotions is unfair and naive.

At the Bowen Walker Foundation, we want to honor the precious lives that have been lost. We want to provide these grieving children with the necessary tools to be proud brothers and sisters. We want to create for them a space, gift them a voice, and instill in them a new level of confidence to keep the memory of their siblings alive forever. Our children deserve so much better than what is available to them. Our children deserve to be able to recognize that two emotions can live together at once. Our children deserve the ability to grieve, the chance to honor, and the tools to survive after the loss of their siblings. If we don't give that to them, who will?

The foundation truly is a family affair. Sawyer and Dawson love to help in any way they possibly can. They talk about things that they received after Bowen's passing that made them feel closer to him. They share their favorite books about emotion, grief, and loss. They collaborate with me on identifying their favorite toys, stuffed animals, and family activities we have done in an attempt to keep Bowen's memory alive. When we prepare a care package to be sent to a new family, they race to color a picture, talking about the new friends Bowen is making in Heaven and how we can pray for the new little boy or girl grieving the loss of their brother or sister.

Each and every single life lost deserves to be remembered. Each baby. Each child. Each sibling. God has called me into a line of work where I live in my grief each and every day; a world where I meet people going through the worst events they will ever encounter, and I meet them when they are and where they are. I pray with them, I cry with them, I love with them. I might not know what I am doing more often than not, but I know that with God, I am never doing it alone. He has placed this calling onto my heart, and I'm choosing to follow Him. I'm choosing His calling over my comfort.

CHAPTER TWENTY-FIVE

A God-Sized Plan

I don't know about you, but I have a tendency to plan every aspect of my life. I'm what you might call "type A." I like to plan, I like to take charge, and unknowns bother me. As kids, we grow up with the idea that we have to have it all together. At a young age, we are conditioned to think about, and plan, where we would like to be in five and ten years. We are asked to imagine where we will be when we graduate high school or college. Our life plans are so frequently mentioned, and oftentimes praised, in our culture, yet they're not really *ours*, are they? When things don't go our way, we blame the universe, or are quick to say, "It wasn't God's plan," but how frequently do we actually trust and follow His plan for us? Instead, we use it as a scapegoat for our own plans failing and falling apart.

Growing up in church, we hear time and time again about God's plan for us. A quick Google search will show you countless verses, passages, and inspirational quotes about His plan for our lives and how to seek out and follow it. On one hand, that seems so easy, right? To give up control and allow God to take over. On the other hand, however, as humans we are a stubborn, selfish people who, if we are being honest with ourselves, like to control things, make plans, and have things go *our* way. We live such chaotic lives in such a chaotic world that oftentimes planning, even for small things, helps create a sense of calm.

As a mother, I know that planning out what my children will wear to school the night before helps the morning rush out the door go so much smoother. Planning a menu for the week lessens the stress of dinner while we rush around doing homework or making it to after-school sports and activities. When we forget to pick out the clothes, pull out the frozen meat for dinner, or pre-pack backpacks, we see the strings holding our chaotic lives start to unravel, creating a sense of panic. When I think about how smoothly my life runs when I have it "all together" versus the days I do not, it is hard to imagine giving up control and trusting His plan for me.

We live in a society obsessed with creating our own truth, with toxic amounts of self-love and righteousness and manifesting without God. We are constantly attempting to create the lives we want for ourselves, regardless of what God's plan is for us. I would be lying if I said I was not guilty of each and every one of these errors. Planning is in my blood, and like John "Hannibal" Smith from *The A-Team* says, "I love it when a plan comes together." If only following God's plan were as easy as it is to make my own.

I am all for a good vision board. In fact, I have one hanging up in my bathroom right now, serving as a reminder to myself every morning of the type of wife, mother, and person I want to be. On it there are Bible verses, inspiring quotes about motherhood, and reminders to exhale and trust Him. So many mornings I walk right past it, not even allowing a glance to fall in its direction. Other times, it stops me in my tracks. A word, a verse, or even a beautiful flower will catch my gaze, reminding me to redirect my focus to the One who created me.

It took me a long time to realize that following God's plan does not mean giving up everything you aspire to be, letting go of your goals, and blindly stepping out into the world hoping He will catch you. Growing up, I always feared that truly following God would look a lot like the people we read about in the Bible: the ones who were asked to give up everything they had, leave everyone they loved, and live a foreign life, in a foreign land, alone with nobody but God to rely on. The idea of doing that scared me to no end, and oftentimes lead me to situations where I tried to barter with God, asking over and over whether or not I should do what I felt Him calling me to, and saying I trusted Him while also making my own "secret" backup plan.

As humans, we desire to see the full, big picture while struggling to see past the tips of our noses. On more occasions than I could honestly count, I have admitted that if I could just see how the future of a situation would play out, then maybe I would be more willing to pick up my cross and follow Him. God knows this about us, just as He knows *everything* about us, and graciously gave us the power of free will for this very reason. He *wants* us to turn and follow him. He *desires* for us to follow Him and His plans for us. It is our choice. While it is often frustrating, difficult, and ominous, I am personally very thankful for this choice. The joy we receive from choosing Him is far greater than anything we could ever receive ourselves. My journey through marriage, motherhood, infertility, miscarriage, and loss paints the most beautiful picture of this. Throughout my life, like many others, I have come to the crossroads between faith and mistrust, the choice between picking up my cross and following Jesus, and turning to walk away completely. The circumstances that led me to those crossroads were never easy; however, the choice, for me personally, was never hard. God never said He would not give us more than we could handle. What He did promise was that we never had to go through it alone, and time and time again He has proven just that to me and my family.

I am no stranger to sharing my testimony. I know there is power in my story and that God gave it to me for a reason. While sharing, I have been told I am "the strongest mom alive," "one of the strongest people I know," and—my personal favorite—something along the lines of "I don't know how you do it, you are so strong." As someone who struggles with diagnosed PTSD, anxiety, and ADHD, I oftentimes find this laughable, especially when I know this "strength" I so frequently exhibit is not from me at all, but through God. Alone, I am a mess of a human. My ducks are never in a row, my ship is probably both on fire and sinking, and I spend the majority of my time coordinating chaos. Life is messy. Marriage is messy. Motherhood is messy. God helps the mess, knows the plan, and lights the path for us.

CHAPTER TWENTY-SIX

A Web of Grace

"We can't see past the tip of our nose, but God sees the whole big picture." I could not even begin to count the number of times I have heard a version of that statement. When you are wading through the waters of the storm, looking past the tip of your nose seems impossible, yet at times it is all you can think about. As Christians, we often are reminded, even through the worst possible situations in our lives, that it is "God's plan." When we don't understand, we are repeatedly told that we might not see it now, but eventually we will.

So many other "Christian sayings" are thrown around through the storms of our lives, and if we are being completely honest with ourselves, they are the absolute *last* things we want to hear. *Especially* in grief. *How is this part of a bigger plan? I don't want to wait, I want to know now.* Not one person I have met through grief has found these "reassurances" comforting; they've instead found them to be harmful to their grief and healing process. We spend our lives wishing we could just see the bigger picture, whether it pertains to the outcome of a job interview, looking past a hard spot in our relationships, or parenthood. We search for puzzle pieces, seeking hints about the bigger picture of it all in an attempt to see the good that is coming our way. We often pray for the quick way out, wish away the pain, and pray for even a glimpse into the bigger picture of our lives. It often isn't until much later, when we are looking back, that we start to see the beautiful tapestry God has created, especially in the moments that we could not possibly fathom would ever be for good.

Looking back on my life as a whole, I can honestly say I have no complaints. I am one of the lucky few to have had a "normal" upbringing. I am the oldest of three girls, my parents are still married, and I grew up as an active member of my church. Growing up in a Christian household, we went to church twice on Sundays and again on Wednesday nights. I was baptized alongside my younger sister in elementary school. I attended Vacation Bible School, participated in Awana, sang in the youth choir, and spent my summers at church camp. I fell in love and married my college sweetheart, and we quickly began to discuss starting our own family. In a way, I was living my very own fairytale. God was in my heart, but if I'm being honest, I was not living for Him. I have always loved Jesus, but for the vast majority of my youth and even into adulthood, I loved *me* more. I had a plan for my life, and that's what I followed. I put me, and so many other things, before Him.

It wasn't until Sawyer was born that I truly started to understand what it meant to live for the Lord. It wasn't until I was alone, on the operating room table, listening to nurses and respiratory therapists try time and time again to revive my son, that my faith came to life. I lay still, listening frantically to medical professionals repeating over and over that there was no heartbeat. In that moment, I could only think of one single thing to do: pray. For the first time in my life, my prayers were different. In that moment, I gave it all to God. All of me, all of my child, all of my marriage was given to God. I let go of what I wanted and instead began to pray that God's will be done. I opened my heart to Jesus, surprising even myself, as I began to cry out to God with gratitude and thanksgiving. My baby, my *son* was not alive, and I was *thanking* God. Truly thanking Him, with all of me, for His will. Each and every word that left my lips that day was the most genuine thing I have ever felt or prayed. I thanked Him for my pregnancy, regardless of the outcome. I thanked Him for each and every nurse, doctor, and therapist in that operating room. I thanked Him for Sawyer, not knowing if I'd ever see my son alive. I prayed that *if* His will was for us to leave the hospital without a baby, that He would give me strength: not only strength for myself, but the strength I would need to tell Zach, who was anxiously waiting in the hospital waiting room, unaware if either of us would make it out of the surgery. I thanked Him for Zach and for our marriage. In those moments of praise and thanksgiving, I felt a true sense of peace beyond my own understanding. A type of peace that only the Lord Himself can provide surrounded me as resuscitation efforts failed, yet continued.

I prayed for Sawyer. I prayed for his life and asked God that if it was His will, he would survive. I prayed that the medical team would not give up on him, and that God would give them the strength and courage to continue trying. Above all my other prayers, however, I continued to thank Him. I know God was in the operating room that night. Every medical professional, hospital staff member, and specialist present that night will tell you the exact same thing. God was there. He saved Sawyer. He breathed life back into my son, 20 minutes after he was born; He gave him new life. He gave *me* a new life. I might have asked Jesus into my heart as a child, but on December 5, 2016, I truly began living my life for God. I knew that no matter what happened, He was in control. God changed me that night, and I am so thankful that I will never be the same.

Seven and a half years of puzzle pieces sit scattered before me, making it hard to ignore God's involvement. His web of grace lies before me, the darkest storms illuminated at each intersection. We experienced a lot of God's miracles. We also experienced a lot of pain, grief, and heartache. I learned more medical terminology than I ever cared to know, and spent far too many hours inside hospitals and doctor's offices.

As humans, Zach and I were constantly scared to death of the unknown. We knew God had gone before us, paving a way, but the road seemed dark, eerie, and painful. We often feared to take the next step, instead of letting Him light the path laid out in front of us. Sawyer was the first baby to ever code at our hospital. Hospital policies were set in place as a direct response to his birth. The ambulance driver who arrived late that December night to transport a sick baby and his dad to a hospital in Atlanta was the same ambulance driver who, six and a half years later, picked up a scared, pregnant mother. He loaded me up and once again drove my son and one of his parents to the hospital where I would later give birth. Back at the first hospital, the room in the NICU that housed Sawyer before he was ultimately transported ended up being the same NICU room that Dawson stayed in during his stay. The nurse who delivered Sawyer was the same nurse who delivered Dawson, and one of the nurses who took care of me when I was pregnant with Bowen before our transfer.

My incision reopened, pushing back my arrival time at the NICU the day Bowen started to decline, allowing me to be present as he underwent his longest and most dangerous surgery. My doctor specifically requested that both Zach and I be present at my appointment the morning of June 20. Zach and I both rearranged our schedules and made our way to an appointment to teach Zach how to pack my wound, and because of that, we were able to be present when Bowen passed. We were able to reroute, arriving at the hospital just five minutes after receiving the phone call. We were able to hold our son while he was still alive, tenderly loving Bowen in his final moments, instead of arriving after it was too late.

Wow. The handiwork of God is so evident throughout our story, I cannot help but sit back and smile. I would be lying if I said I recognized His hand through every aspect of my life, or that I could think about the world past the tip of my nose, much less wait for it. Through pain, grief, and confusion, it is so easy to overlook God's merciful hand in each of these moments, but as a Christian, I can't help but see the beauty in these gracious works of God. Sawyer and Dawson sharing the same room in the NICU brought peace in a time of frustration. Being transported by the same EMT as Sawyer brought comfort through the unknown. Raising money for the NICU brought my family joy, but finding out that our son, over two years later, was directly affected by the generosity that day brought solace. It is not lost on me that my C-section incision reopened *so that* Zach and I would be there when Bowen passed.

These illustrations, even through moments of pain, tragedy, and trauma, show me that God is still present. It is so easy to overlook His role and presence in these moments. It is so easy to get angry. To get frustrated or upset, because you feel alone. You feel as if He is not there. In those moments, I can assure you, He is standing right by your side. He has paved a way for you, and in the moments of sorrow and grief, where you are heartbroken and feel so alone, He is right beside you. He is holding you. He is weeping with you. I often think back to when Lazarus died in the Bible. Jesus wept. He *knew* He was about to raise him from the dead. He *knew* that in just a few moments, he would be alive again, reunited with his family. Even with the ability to see the bigger picture, He wept. His love for Mary and Martha and Lazarus outweighed what was to come. God sent Jesus to earth to experience human emotion and suffering. Hebrews 4:15 tells us that He experienced temptation, understands our emotions, and feels our pain. He experienced trauma and grief, and because of all of those things He is able to relate to us, not only in our joy, but in our heartache as well.

The number of God moments that have taken place over the last seven and a half years of my life is can't be ignored. I know that He has wept when I have wept. He has rejoiced when I have rejoiced, and He has held me when I was unable to hold myself up. "With all your family has gone through, how do you still have faith in God?": a question I have been asked so many times I have lost count. Regularly, people ask how I can see God, trusting Him through pain and tragedy. They often want to know how I have been able to remain faithful, even growing in my faith, through the loss of our son. If I'm being honest, I don't understand how people can do this without Him. I *know* that I am the woman I am today because of God. I *know* that I am able to get up every single morning and be a mother, wife, and friend because of the strength God gives me. I *know* that while my time with Bowen on earth was cut way too short, nothing will compare to the eternity that I *know* I will be able to spend with him in Heaven.

Love and grief walk hand in hand. We have grief because we have love, and I choose to thank God for Bowen now in the same way I thanked Him the day I found out I was pregnant again. I choose to thank God for the years of infertility we experienced because it allowed me to grow, maturing into the person I am now, so that I might live out my loss in the way that I am. I am thankful that every piece of my life's puzzle, every storm, and every moment woven together have created the most beautiful story of life, loss, and love, allowing me to honor and glorify Him.

Am I thankful that Bowen passed? Absolutely not. I will never understand. I will never stop missing him or grieving his loss. What I am thankful for, however, is the ability to serve a God who promises everything works together for the good of His will and Kingdom. I am thankful to serve a God who promises I *will* see Bowen again. I am thankful for the platform that I have been given so that I might touch the lives of others who, unfortunately, are experiencing the same pain that my family has.

While we can't see the big picture right away, and oftentimes we get frustrated hearing about God's plan through trauma and grief and pain, being able to look back, connect the dots, and see His work in our lives firsthand is one of the most beautiful things I have ever been able to do. Not only does it help me feel connected to those who are now gone, living before His presence in Heaven, but it also helps me to feel connected to God. In moments where I question His presence and love for me, I am able to look back and see that I've never been alone. I'm able to see that He has never left me. He has never abandoned me. I'm able to perceive a connection, watching the puzzle pieces come together, and see His plan in a way that I had never been able to before. Through Sawyer's birth, He paved a way for his life and story. Through Dawson's birth, He paved a way for our family to continue to grow and trust in Him. Through my ectopic pregnancy, we were able to place one foot in front of the other, knowing He walked alongside us. During our battle with infertility, He gently guided us. As we experienced Bowen's pregnancy, birth, and death, He carried us. On a path much too difficult to walk alone, He scooped us up in His arms, cried as we cried, and carried us down the road.

One of the last things I was able to tell Bowen was that I was proud of him. He has taught our entire family so much about life, love, loss, and faith. Never once did I question God's love for me or our family. Did I ask why? Absolutely! Was I angry? More than ever. But did I wonder if He loved us? Never. Our faith is why we are all still here today. Without God, I can say without a shadow of a doubt that I would not still be here. Sawyer would not be here. Dawson would not be here. My marriage would not still be fruitful and thriving. You see, *the presence of pain does not mean the absence of God.* If you had told me ten years ago that I would experience all that I have in my journey through fertility and motherhood, I would have asked why you'd wish such a grim fate on me, but looking back, I don't see it that way at all. God is using me. He didn't "curse" me, but instead is using me, through my own tragedy and heartbreak, to bring others to Him.

I have always believed that if God brought you to it, He would bring you through it. I have learned along the way, though, that you might not like His methods or modes of transportation. The bridge might be frail and creaky, with boards missing and ropes fraying. The waves might be tall and mighty, rocking the boat a little bit harder than you are comfortable with. The gas tank might look like it is about to run out, leaving you stranded on the side of an abandoned highway. The journey is confusing. The directions seem to be translated into a different language, and you struggle to find which way is up.

No matter how the circumstances might seem, I know He will carry me through. I trust His plan. With Him, I safely cross the bridge to the other side. My boat does not capsize, leaving me to drown alone at sea. My car safely makes it to my destination. I remain strong. I remain faithful. I know He is with me to the end.

CHAPTER TWENTY-SEVEN

One Mother of a Miracle

I have never had a normal birth. In fact, I really haven't ever had a normal labor. I know you're probably thinking, what is a "normal" labor and delivery experience? What would I even consider normal? While I agree that every individual labor and birth story is unique and special in its own way, the end goal is always a healthy baby. Most people, when they go into the hospital to give birth, are anticipating going home with that baby. Not many people go in with the anticipation of a NICU stay. Not many people go in with the knowledge or understanding that they won't go home with their baby.

Before Sawyer was born, this was my anticipation, too. While nervous, I was eager and excited to be able to finally hold my baby in my arms. I longed for the first cry, the matching outfits in the hospital, and sharing hundreds of pictures with our family and friends. I never anticipated having to break the news to our family that our son might not make it. I never imagined the possibility of my newborn being taken from me, before I ever was able to hold or touch him, and being sent to a different hospital. A hospital that I was not at. I never imagined that the day I gave birth, I would be alone in the hospital, without my son or my husband, because they were an hour away at a different hospital. The night Sawyer was born, I waited anxiously by my phone, not knowing if my son survived transport. I anxiously waited to hear from Zach, knowing he may be faced with the impossible decision to discontinue life support on his own, or that we might have to make the decision together, yet separated, over the phone.

Sawyer. My brainiac. My athlete. He excels at math and loves going to school more than any kid I have ever met. He is extremely skilled when it comes to karate, football, and soccer. He is a rule-follower to his very core and loves his mama fiercely. The world's best big brother.

When I was in labor with Dawson, I was cautiously optimistic for a healing labor and delivery. What happened to Sawyer was a "one-off," and we were doing everything possible to ensure that it did not happen again. When the nurse put him on my chest, I felt a giant wave of relief wash over me, but before I could even really grasp what was happening, he was gone. Surely he didn't actually need to go to the NICU as well, right? Wrong. I waited in denial for him to be brought back to my room perfectly fine for the entire day after he was born, fully convinced that I couldn't possibly have two NICU babies. The day I was discharged, knowing once again that I had to leave my son, was when the reality really set in. I watched all the other moms being wheeled out with their babies while I left, once again, with empty arms.

Dawson. My free spirit. We have always said he doesn't dance to the beat of his own drum, but instead is off in the corner playing the tambourine. He brings so much laughter and joy to our home. He has a heart of gold, is as smart as a whip, and feels all the feelings in the best way possible.

When I first found out I was pregnant with Bowen, I immediately said my goal was to have a NICU-free stay. After all, what were the odds that I would have not one, not two, but *three* NICU babies, right? Upon admittance to the hospital after my water broke so early, my tone immediately changed. I knew that if I was lucky, there would be a NICU stay. A NICU stay meant the chance of life, and I shifted my prayers from a healthy, uneventful delivery to a long, successful NICU stay. This didn't make anything easier, though. Going through the neonatal motions for the third time was the hardest part yet. Talking to doctors, nurses, and respiratory therapists about survival rates, outcomes, and care plans for the third time was exhausting on a whole new level. My heart was tired, my body was exhausted, and while I understood on a technical level so much of what they were talking about from our first two stays, I also knew that no two babies were the same. No two likelihoods had the same outcomes, and just because we had walked a similar path before, did not mean we were in for the same journey.

Leaving Bowen at the hospital was by far the hardest of the three. He was the most critical. He was the smallest by a long shot, and we were also farther from the hospital than ever before. With Sawyer, I was given a small room with an uncomfortable twin-sized bed, and I never left. While I was not physically with my son, I was just a short walk down the hall. With Dawson, we lived less than ten minutes from the hospital, and I spent the majority of my days with him. However, with Bowen, we lived over 45 minutes away. I could not stay, and we could not get there quickly if we needed to. Each time we left the hospital, I cried, held my breath, and constantly checked my phone for any updates from the hospital. Every morning when I woke up, evening when we got home, and night before bed, I called to check on him. I made sure my phone was always on loud and jumped every time it made a noise.

Bowen. My angel. My tiny fighter. From before he was even born, he had a personality bigger than this world. He was strong. He was feisty. He fought for us harder than we could ever have asked him to. His legacy reaches further than we could ever have imagined. My tiny, perfect, amazing, baby.

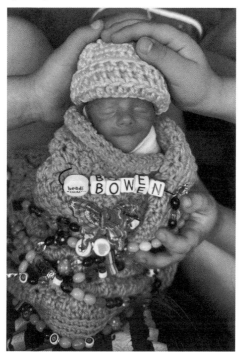

I've never had a normal birth experience. I have trauma, layers of it. I have never been wheeled out of the hospital holding my baby. I have never given my baby their first bath, taken precious newborn pictures in the hospital with them, or even announced a healthy birth. Instead, I have more medical knowledge than I ever thought I would. I have tiny blood pressure cuffs, NICU wristbands, and graduation certificates. I have a box with memorial items and phone numbers for counselors specializing in PTSD, grief, and trauma. I have caseworkers and so much pain. I often joke that I have no clue what to do with a newborn. I couldn't tell you what to do with an umbilical cord, how much or for how long an infant is supposed to eat, or what the "golden hour" after birth even is. I have held my friends' babies younger than I was ever able to hold any of my own, a privilege that has never been lost on me.

One mother. Three miracles. This is my story of faith, love, hope, miracles, death, grief, and a whole lot of God. Sawyer, Dawson, and Bowen. My three babies. My three gifts from God. I will never understand *why* I was chosen to be Sawyer's mom, or Dawson's, or Bowen's. I will never understand why He called Bowen home, or what His plan is for our lives. What I do know is that He is *still* good. In the good, He is good. In the bad, He is good. Even in the unimaginable, He is *good*, and because of that, I will spend the rest of my life in pursuit of Him and His Kingdom. One step at a time. One Heavenly Father. One Mother of a Miracle.

Acknowledgments

I want to thank all the people who helped make this book a possibility:

I would first like to thank the **One** who truly made this possible, our Heavenly Father. His grace, mercy, and love has carried me not only through my journey as an author, but through my journey as a mother. All my praise goes to Him as I share my story with the world.

To my amazing husband, **Zach**. You never once doubted me, even when I doubted myself. Thank you for all your hard work and everything you do for me and our boys. From taking on more responsibilities at home so I could write, to staying up late to help read and review sections, you have always been my biggest cheerleader. I could not have done this without you. I love you!

To my boys, **Sawyer** and **Dawson**, thank you for your patience, honesty, and love as mommy has written this book. Hearing you are proud of me gives me the courage to keep going. Keep shining your lights for Jesus! To **Bowen**, thank you for being our guardian angel, and showing me how to be brave. I love all three of you so much!

To my family, I would like to say thank you for always believing in me. My parents, **Jeff** and **Jenny**, have always supported and loved me, and writing this book has been no different. My sisters, **Jessie** and **Rachel**, have always encouraged me to succeed. Knowing I have made the four of you proud means the world to me.

To my closest friends, thank you for never leaving me, for holding me, for crying with me, and for helping pick up the pieces along the way. To **Kayla**, my platonic soulmate, thank you for the last almost 20 years of friendship. Thank you for being by my side through all four pregnancies, for leaving a contract to be by my side after Bowen passed, and for everything in between. To **Amber**, thank you for being my other half. You are the rock in my village and have carried me more than you know. Thanks for being my mascot for life and for giving me sweet A.Z. to love on through my grief. To **Annie**, thank you for always being my sounding board. Thank you for your constant prayer and encouragement, and for always knowing what I need—even when I don't want to admit I need it myself. To **Morgan**, thank you for your vulnerability through grief. I know I am safe to share my heart around you, no matter how whacky it might sound saying it out loud. I love you all immensely.

To **Dr. Barrett**, our family would not be the same without you. Thank you for never giving up on us. Thank you for saving Sawyer's life. The world would be a much better place if people were more like you. We love you.

To **Brandy**, from Sawyer's birth, Dawson's pregnancy and birth, my ectopic pregnancy, battling infertility and Bowen's pregnancy and birth, you have always been by my side. Thank you. I know God sent you to my room the night Sawyer was born for a reason, and I am so thankful He did. You mean the world to us.

To both the past and present **Northeast Georgia Medical Center Braselton and Gainseville Labor and Delivery and NICU staff**, thank you for all the love, energy, and care you poured into not only my three boys, but Zach and myself as well. I know we have kept you on your toes since 2016, and we could not be more thankful for each and every one of you. Special thanks to Robin Rutledge, Angela Powell, Joel Martin, Davalyn Ball, Tammy LaMar, Amy Weldon, Dr. Martin, Ellen

Wren, Dr. Harrison, Liz Griffin, Dr. Tadros, Noël Padgett, Carley Allen, Paige Furlan, Kassi Turpin, Rebecca Nave, Sarah Parker, Lydia George, Ashley McKinnon, Elizabeth Ward, Kathryn Nowak, Alexis Williams, Dr. Ward, Lori Valentine, Karen Hoyt, Mandy Reichert, Renee Chambers, Judi Dailey, Dr. Coto-Puckett, Katelyn Hopkins, Dr. Cabrera, Claire Sides, Rebecca Thompson, Dr. Castillo, Lilia Ponizhaylo, and in special memory of Stephanie Ellis. You have all left a lasting impact on our lives, and we are forever grateful.

To **Holly Mock** and **Langley Courchaine**, thank you for taking care of us, feeding us, and picking us up more times than I can count this past year and a half. God weaved you perfectly into our lives and we are so incredibly blessed by His perfect addition of you both to our family. We love you!

To **Bowen Walker Foundation** supporters, families, and donors, thank you for believing in us. Being able to cultivate a community through sibling loss has been so special and I am honored to walk hand-in-hand with others on their grief journey.

To the team at Blue Hat Publishing, **Brandon**, **Tim**, and **Rachael**, thank you for believing in me and my story from day one. Special thanks to **Jodi Sherwood** for holding my hand throughout this journey. Your love and support mean the world to me. Thank you!